BETHLEHEM SPEAKS

BETHLEHEM SPEAKS

Voices from the little town cry out

Garth Hewitt

First published in Great Britain in 2008

Society for Promoting Christian Knowledge
36 Causton Street
London SW1P 4ST

The author and publisher have made every effort to ensure that the
external website and email addresses included in this book are correct
and up to date at the time of going to press. The author and publisher
are not responsible for the content, quality or continuing accessibility
of the sites.

Unless otherwise noted, Scripture quotations are taken from the New Revised
Standard Version of the Bible, Anglicized Edition, copyright © 1989, 1995
by the Division of Christian Education of the National Council of the
Churches of Christ in the USA. Used by permission. All rights reserved.

Every effort has been made to seek permission to use copyright
material reproduced in this book. The publisher apologizes for those
cases where permission might not have been sought and, if notified,
will formally seek permission at the earliest opportunity.

British Library Cataloguing-in-Publication Data
A catalogue record for this book is available from the British Library

ISBN 978–0–281–05956–0

1 3 5 7 9 10 8 6 4 2

Typeset by Graphicraft Ltd, Hong Kong
Printed in Great Britain by CPI Bookmarque, Croydon

Produced on paper from sustainable forests

Dedicated to my Palestinian godchildren
from Beit Sahour – Leah Ann and Sarah

May the future bring you
justice, peace and a joyful hope

Contents

Contents

Acknowledgements

The words and music of the songs 'Hidden from view', 'They've cancelled Christmas (The wall must fall)', 'Candle of hope', 'Humans too', 'Shine on', 'One of us' are written by Garth Hewitt © Chain of Love Music, administered by Daybreak Music Ltd, PO Box 2848, Eastbourne BN20 7XP.

The publisher and author acknowledge with thanks permission to reproduce extracts from the following:

On page xi, *The Cure at Troy: A Version of Sophocles' Philoctetes* by Seamus Heaney, published by Farrar, Straus & Giroux, New York, 1991.

On page 114, the poem 'A prayer for peace', by John O'Donohue, from *Benedictus: A Book of Blessings*, published by Bantam Press, London, 2007. Reprinted by permission of the Random House Group Ltd.

On page 128, the poem 'Advent' by John Betjeman.

Introduction

Human beings suffer,
They torture one another,
They get hurt and get hard.
No poem or play or song
Can fully right a wrong
Inflicted and endured.

. . .

History says, don't hope
On this side of the grave.
But then, once in a life time
The longed-for tidal wave
Of justice can rise up,
And hope and history rhyme.

So hope for a great sea-change
On the far side of revenge.
Believe that a further shore
Is reachable from here.
Believe in miracle
And cures and healing wells . . .

Seamus Heaney (from The Cure at Troy,
Farrar, Straus & Giroux, 1991)

A terrible crime is happening in a land once known as holy.
Palestinians are under siege. As I write this, Gaza is completely
under siege and a major humanitarian crisis has developed. Basic
human rights are being denied, particularly rights to decent

living conditions, health and education. On 19 September 2007, the Israeli government declared the Gaza Strip a 'hostile entity' and has stepped up its collective punishment. This crime, which has been perpetrated against civilians, violates international law and the fourth Geneva Convention. Again, at the time of writing this, Israel has been invading both Gaza and the West Bank day after day and carrying out targeted assassinations which resulted during a three-week period (3–23 January 2008, according to the Palestinian Centre for Human Rights) in the killing of 71 people and the injuring of 239. Also right across the West Bank Israel is involved in large numbers of kidnappings. In the first half of January 100 were kidnapped according to the General League of Palestinian Workers. One day, during the week beginning 20 January 2008, 20 people were kidnapped from Nablus. These people will be added to the number of around 10,000 people being held in jail by the Israelis where they can be subjected not only to imprisonment but also to torture.

In this book, however, I will not be focusing on what is happening in Gaza or in the northern West Bank but looking mainly at the area of the three Christian towns of Bethlehem, Beit Sahour and Beit Jala.

The 'little town of Bethlehem' has been shrunk and strangled over the last few years, but though it has happened right under our noses, most people outside have not even noticed.

At Christmas all around the world, a third of the world's population sing about the 'little town of Bethlehem'. Yet for most there is no concept of the reality of what is happening to the community of Bethlehem who are under siege, economically strangled, with a very large percentage of their land taken. In fact 87 per cent of Bethlehem's land has now been taken, and the wall, which is sometimes called the 'security barrier', has been a key aspect of taking land. If it was indeed a security barrier, it would have been built along the 1967 border or green line. But in fact it swoops in and out of the West Bank, going in for many miles and taking as much land as possible, often fertile land, thereby cutting people off from the place where they work, that is, their fields. A town like Qalqilya is completely surrounded by the wall and now the Bethlehem area is surrounded by a series of walls that imprison the people. It is like a medieval siege and being inside this siege is like stepping back in time. You have that shocking sense that one group of people, because of their race, is not acceptable to the world. The word *hafrada* is used to describe the wall in Hebrew; it means 'separation'. This is clearly what the wall is meant to achieve – both separation and segregation.

The level of depression there is overwhelming and, when I went to write this book, I was taken aback at the utter devastation that is happening to this community. For too long, there has been much beating around the bush in terms of speaking up about the Israeli–Palestinian conflict. Often terms are used that suggest that the two sides are equal, with very little concept that it is a situation of 'oppressor' and 'oppressed', 'occupier' and 'occupied'.

Likewise there is very little concept of the impact of the wall. First of all, its size is nearly nine metres high and, second, its length, either as wall or fence, is approximately 470 kilometres around the West Bank already and is planned to be about 750 kilometres; that is far higher and far longer than the Berlin Wall. The impact of this statistic, however, is even more devastating as, in our time and perhaps hidden from our gaze, a whole community is being destroyed – cut off from one another, cut off from the outside world, and cut off from employment possibilities in Israel.

Bethlehem is only five miles or so from Jerusalem. This was their natural link where people would go both to worship and to shop and to meet friends. Most have not been able to go now for many years. There has been a deliberate cutting them off from Jerusalem.

I have written three books about the situation in Palestine and Israel, namely *Pilgrims and Peacemakers*, *Candle of Hope* and *Towards the Dawn*. This is not an attempt to write a more complete book like one of those, but to update the situation in *Towards the Dawn*. Because that was published in 2004, it is now out of date on the situation of the wall. The interviews with people, be they Christians, Jews or Muslims, are still very important and give an insight into the peacemakers of various communities, and this book is meant to sit alongside *Towards the Dawn* and to provide resource material for churches. It does not interview Jewish Israelis or Muslims, as in *Towards the Dawn*, as it focuses specifically on the Christians of Bethlehem; this book is intended as a call to the churches to wake up to what is happening to the Christian towns of Bethlehem, Beit Sahour and Beit Jala, and the impact on the Christian community there. In this book the 16 witnesses are all Christians; it does have some Israeli voices, but they are Arab Palestinians from among the 20 per cent minority in Israel. I quote Rabbi Jeremy Milgrom at one point, who has a very close Muslim friend in one of the refugee camps inside Bethlehem. But Jewish Israeli citizens are no longer allowed to travel into Bethlehem and the West Bank, thus pushing the communities further apart – another worrying aspect of what is going on.

Every time I have written a book about the Holy Land, I have hoped and prayed that by the time it was published, the situation would be more peaceful and that it would therefore be out of date. In every single case, it has always been worse. I still hope and pray that things will change. We have just recently

(January 2008) heard President George W. Bush calling for an end to occupation and for returning to the 1967 borders. However, immediately after both the Annapolis conference and George Bush's visits, the Israelis have continued their invasions, assassinations and kidnappings and also the building of settlements, which the president asked them to stop. George Bush suggested that there could be peace in a year. I hope by the time you read this that that has become a reality, but I fear that another story altogether may have happened. This book is written, though, still hoping that a journey will have been made towards justice and peace for the Palestinians and security and peace for the Israelis.

I work with the Amos Trust, an organization committed to human rights, motivated by the belief that all are of equal value because all are made in the image of God. We have partners in Gaza, Israel and the West Bank and we work with Christians, Jews and Muslims and those who are not necessarily from a faith community, and we learn from them all. Amos's approach to working in Israel/Palestine is basically summed up as, 'We are committed to win/win for both communities, which can only be achieved by peace with justice and equal rights for all.'

I hope that in our time we will be privileged to see and experience in the land once called holy what Seamus Heaney talks about as 'The longed-for tidal wave of justice'. May it become a reality that brings 'a great sea-change on the far side of revenge'.

The most important section of this book is contained in Chapters 4 to 6 – the voices of 16 witnesses. In my two visits in May and October 2007 I interviewed a variety of Christians from the Bethlehem area and a few from Jerusalem and Nazareth.

Some people I interviewed are left out for technical reasons (i.e. problem with the taping!) or, as in the case of Bishop Suheil Dawani, I became ill and pressed the wrong button and he was cut off in mid flow. I then retreated to clinics, doctors and cardiologists to be sorted out! It meant I left early on my first visit.

My thanks to Wisam and Rasha Salsaa, Zoughbi Zoughbi and all at Wi'am, to all I interviewed who were so patient with me, Sue and Simon Plater, who took over leading our Amos group when I had to return home. Sue and Simon then came out again with my wife Gill on the second trip. Thanks to Christy Reiners who started typing up interviews for me and Kari Stewart who took over; also to Sarah Dean at Amos who did some typing and much planning. To Chris Rose who looked after everything at Amos as I disappeared to write this.

Garth Hewitt

1

Humans too

——◆◆◆——

Humans too
I've got some news – may be a surprise
It's a basic truth I've come to recognize
May come as a shock – it's only known to a few
But Palestinians are humans too.

If you share this secret – if you say it loud
You're gonna be criticized without any doubt
'Cos they're hated and despised, and denied their rights
But strangely they're precious in God's own eyes.

Palestinians are humans too
They weep and they bleed like me and like you
We can treat them like outcasts as so many do
But Palestinians are humans too.

Garth Hewitt

'We should genuflect in front of each one'

Just before I went to Bethlehem to research the material for this book I was invited to a service at Lancing College by my niece Charlotte Dedman who is a student there. It was to hear Archbishop Desmond Tutu speak at a special service to dedicate a stained-glass window to the memory of Archbishop

Trevor Huddleston (who had also attended Lancing College). Archbishop Tutu reminisced about the struggle against apartheid and talked about the value of each human being. He said human beings are so important because they are 'God carriers', 'they are tabernacles', 'carriers of the Holy Spirit'. 'We should genuflect in front of each one like we do in front of the reserved sacrament.' He talked of Huddleston's God as 'notoriously biased in favour of the poor, the downtrodden and those without clout'. These words kept going through my mind as I saw how people were treated in Palestine. Palestinians were 'non-people' – the wrong race, powerless, being hidden from view behind a monstrous wall of inhumanity – yet Tutu had reminded us that we should 'genuflect in front of each person'. Here in the birthplace of Jesus we need to rediscover again the value of each human being made 'in the image of God'.

Security is the word used to cover a multitude of sins by the Israelis. Yet there seems to be no concept that the Palestinians deserve security too. In everything I write, I write from the basic assumption that human beings are equal, that there should be peace and security for both communities, and I simply do not believe that you can achieve peace and security for one without peace and security for the other. So as I plead for justice for the appallingly treated Palestinians; I believe in the long run to treat them with dignity and justice will show the way to peace for Israelis too.

For too long leaders have been quiet. Political leaders such as Tony Blair have apparently been shocked, according to news reports, by what they have seen when they go to Palestine, especially regarding the wall and the shape of the occupation which on the ground is so clearly an imprisonment. But when he was in power, he must have received this information all the time, so it is a little hard to understand why he and other political leaders are so shocked. Perhaps it is seeing it first-hand that brings home the reality, which is not so strong when it is on paper.

Religious leaders also have been hesitant to speak up. It was very good that Archbishop Rowan Williams and other church leaders went to visit Bethlehem at Christmas 2006. It was an encouragement to people, but there has been very little publicity since. People were delighted that they came, and the religious leaders promised to stand with them. I know there have been follow-ups, but on the ground when you ask people, few are aware of them.

At Christmas 2007, there was no news in the press of religious leaders going to Bethlehem, but Banksy and other artists went and opened their Santa's Ghetto shop in Manger Square and brought far more publicity worldwide, thereby making a prophetic witness with humour and publicity. I will include in the book the story of Tawfiq Salsaa's walled nativity, which caused a stir around the world. A man who has worked for years in olive wood expressed something of his frustration of what was happening in his home town and this simple gesture spoke with enormous power; this story too was carried by the press around the world. So voices are not all silent, and some of the voices of Bethlehem and Palestine will be heard in this book.

They promised to take our land . . . and they took it

When I saw what imprisonment meant in the three square miles of Bethlehem when I was there recently, I realized the world must no longer keep silent. The Church must no longer keep silent. Politicians must face up to their responsibilities under international law. When we look back in history, we may wonder how people kept silent when great injustices were happening. We are living in a context where one is happening

Cravin's Brother & Talented family

in our time, and it will be no good in thirty years' time simply apologizing to the Palestinians; it is happening now and maybe we can do something about it.

Ex-President Jimmy Carter warned the world in 2006, with his book *Palestine: Peace or Apartheid*, that the situation is getting too dangerous to ignore and was drifting terrifyingly towards apartheid. Talking with people in Bethlehem, some of them said simply, 'It is worse than apartheid.' Talking to a black leader from Soweto whom I had worked with against apartheid years ago in South Africa and whom I met after he had just come from Rafah in Gaza, he said, 'This is far worse than apartheid.' Israelis talk of *hafrada*, 'separation', and that is exactly what the Afrikaans word *apartheid* means.

But this word *apartheid* offends some people and there are differences from the apartheid system as it was practised in South Africa, and I certainly do not care what language we use as long as we recognize what is happening on the ground: settlement colonies have been built that are not available to live in if you are Palestinian. Roads have been built that you are not allowed to travel if you are Palestinian. Townships of South Africa did not have walls around them, even though they were tightly controlled. In fact, I do not think apartheid is necessarily the best analogy. I think, along with Zoughbi Zoughbi, our Amos partner from Bethlehem, that probably the best analogy is that of the Native American reservations. I keep returning to Dee Brown's book, *Bury My Heart at Wounded Knee* (Pan Books, 1974), which is the story of the dehumanizing of the Native American people between 1860 and 1889 over years of broken promises, disillusionment, war and massacre. Dee Brown quotes Chief Red Cloud of the Oglala Teton Sioux who said, 'The white man made us many promises, more than I can remember, but they never kept but one; they promised to take our land, and they took it.' This is what we see happening in Palestine.

Why Bethlehem?

One of the questions that I have asked several people has been, why Bethlehem? Why have the Israelis particularly targeted the Bethlehem area and the Christian community? (I am aware that it may not have been as bad as the targeting of Gaza, Nablus, Jenin, Qalqilya or Hebron but nevertheless it has been very deliberate and debilitating.) Mitri Raheb has said in his interview that it is because it is 'the soul of Palestine'. This is why I think of the phrase 'Bury my heart in Bethlehem', which I put in the song lyric 'Hidden from view'. There is something very special in Bethlehem that is being destroyed. I have asked Christians why they feel they especially are being targeted, and with one voice they answer, 'It is because Israel wants the conflict to look as if it is between Jew and Muslim, in which case it believes the West and Christians will come in on the side of the Israelis.' I do not know if that is the way Israel has strategized its attacks of the Bethlehem area, but I have not found anyone who disagrees with that analysis inside the Bethlehem area. I have also found total agreement between Christian and Muslim on this analysis.

Curiously when we issued a press release that the Tawfiq Salsaa walled nativity was available (see Chapter 3), we received some critical emails from Britain and especially from the United States. These critical emails were claiming that the problem for the Christian Palestinians was that they were being attacked by Muslims, and that it was nothing to do with the Israeli occupation. Anyone who has walked on the ground in the Bethlehem areas knows this to be patently untrue. In fact, for years I have suggested the Bethlehem area and indeed all of Palestine as a model for relationships between Christian and Muslim. The same week that we were receiving that criticism, a Muslim organization in Britain called Friends of Al-Aqsa released their second leaflet about 'Christians in Palestine'. The leaflet is a strong support from the Muslim community for the Christians in Palestine and a recognition of their value in that community. It is not to say that, as tensions get greater, there will not be individual conflicts between some people who happen to be Christian and some people who happen to be Muslim; it is however conflict created by the intense pressure cooker in which people now have to live. For instance, as we know from Amos Trust's partner in Bethlehem, Wi'am, the conflict resolution centre, domestic violence has been on the rise because displaced anger is coming out because of the impact of the siege, and it happens between families too.

Religious leaders need to address this more directly. Church leaders are often fearful to speak about it in case they are called 'anti-Semitic'. The truth is, we all need to check our own motives and see if we are anti-Semitic. The history of the Christian Church through the centuries has been appalling and it has led to attacks on Jewish people in Europe, especially after Good Friday services, later the pogroms, and eventually to the Holocaust. Christians have to face our own historic past. At the same time, it is no good patronizing Israelis and Jewish people, because another Semitic group of people is now suffering and we have to reject anti-Semitism, whether against Jew or Arab. It was European Christians who caused the suffering to the Jewish people. To push all that blame on to the Arab world, particularly the Palestinians, is not a way forward for human rights and dignity, nor, for that matter, for peace. Bishara Awad, the Principal of Bethlehem Bible College, said to me:

> Of course the Holocaust was the most evil thing that ever happened. But we need all of us to remember, and especially those who are in a position of leadership, that the Palestinians had nothing to do with the Holocaust. They

are victims. They happened to be here in this land when the Jews decided that this was the God-given land for them and they pushed the Palestinians out. So the Palestinians are in actuality really paying the price for the Holocaust, but they are innocent people as far as the Holocaust is concerned.

I was listening to Chief Rabbi Jonathan Sacks on Holocaust Memorial Sunday (27 January 2008), when he spoke about the lessons to learn from the Holocaust: 'Don't stand by' and 'defend the defenceless'. This it seems to me is the way forward for making sure all are treated fairly and that such terrible events do not happen again.

So, archbishops and rabbis, imams and people of all faiths need to speak up, making sure that they call for justice in this situation, and that they affirm the dignity, humanity and rights of all. All that is being asked for here is that all be treated equally, all be allowed to be free, all to have justice – 'to do unto others as we would have them do to us'. This surely is at the heart of all religions, and our failure to preach and live this may well be at the heart of some of the criticisms of religion that have recently raised their head, not least in Christopher Hitchens' book *God Is Not Great* (Atlantic Books, 2007). It is time we allowed our faiths to be seen as 'great' again because they affirm great principles, great humanity and great justice.

Occupation

But the cause of the problem lies in the one word 'occupation'. If the occupation and the siege were lifted, then the traumatized communities could get back to normal living. So this book is a heartfelt cry and a reminder that unless we solve the situation of the Palestinians, which has gone on since 1948, we cannot reduce the pressure of violence and so-called terrorism in the world.

Unless we deal with this issue, security in our own societies, be that in Britain or the United States, remains as much an issue as it does in Israel. Every time Israel pounds the Palestinians and denies them their human rights, we become more vulnerable. We are all implicated in this. The United Nations is guilty for promising a state for Palestine but never delivering. Sixty years on, it only appears further away. Sixty years on, the biggest group of refugees in the world remains uncompensated. Sixty years on the Palestinians are punished even though they are the victims. Britain is also responsible along with the USA and the EU in failing to be proactive for international law, and not least in the rejection of democracy and the collective punishment that was imposed when Hamas won the election.

Chris Doyle, the Director of the Council for Arab–British Understanding, talking about the treatment of Gaza, stated:

> It is an incredible situation to find that an entire civilian population is openly being abused for political purposes by the government of Israel. The concept of collectively punishing an entire civilian population is simply shocking, but even more so is the limp reaction of key international players, including Britain. Moreover, it is clear that this will not only worsen the conflict, prolong the suffering of both sides and endanger any attempts to push forward negotiations.

How strange that Palestinians in their call for democracy pointed out that they were upset with the corruption in the Palestinian Authority and found a way to express this. But they were punished for it because that was not the choice that the western world wanted. President George W. Bush has played with words like 'freedom' and 'democracy', but if you are really going to be committed to democracy, there are sometimes groups that get into power that you do not like, but you work with them and move to the next stage – that is democracy.

Every hint that Hamas gave in the early days of coming to power was that they would accept the 1967 borders. In 1947 the United Nations gave Israel 55 per cent of the land and Palestine 45 per cent, even though population-wise the Palestinians were larger in numbers than the Israelis at that time. However, in the conflict of 1948–1949, Israel took more land, and at the end of that conflict they controlled 78 per cent of the land. In 1967, when they took the other 22 per cent, what is described as 'the occupation' started.

Yet a remarkable thing happened: the Palestinians have made the most generous offer that one could imagine. At the unsuccessful Camp David meetings organized by President Clinton, they were prepared to give away 78 per cent of their land and make a deal. Barak (then Prime Minister of Israel, now Defence Minister) refused to go with that, and now Israel is in the position where only about 12–15 per cent of the original mandated land is being offered to Palestinians and it is neither contiguous nor viable.

Every Arab state as well as the Palestinian Authority have agreed to accept Israel if it will agree to the 78 per cent of the land. It is a generous offer that lies on the table ready to be taken up at any time. Even Hamas said they would work to this and offered a 40-year *hudna* (truce), during which they would be prepared to talk about it with Israel. The ruthless policy of Sharon (who became Prime Minister of Israel) since 29 September 2000, when he marched with hundreds of soldiers on to the Temple Mount (the Haram al Sharif), has caused the death of around 5,000 Palestinians and around 1,000 Israelis. It has only led to a worse situation and has proved the complete failure of violence as a solution. World politicians need to accept there is a generous solution on the table that can lead to the building of neighbourliness between the two states and an economic community in the Middle East that can join the twenty-first century.

2

Hidden from view

Hidden from view
Hidden from view – hidden from view
Every dream – broken in two
The little town's a prison – the wall keeps them in
Bury my heart at Bethlehem
Where everyone's hidden from view
Forgotten and hidden from view

Hidden from view – hidden from view
Hollow eyes betrayed and confused
The land has been stolen – so have the trees
So has the water – so has the peace
Even Christmas is hidden from view
Everyone's hidden from view

Hidden from view – hidden from view
Your children will ask you, 'What did you do
When they made a ghetto of Bethlehem?
Did you keep silent when the soldiers came
When they built the wall of shame?
Were you just hidden from view?'

Hidden from view – hidden from view
Voices from the ghetto – calling to you

Bethlehem Speaks

Herod is back in control again
Children are suffering in Bethlehem
Where everyone's hidden from view
Forgotten and hidden from view

Hidden from view – hidden from view
Every dream is broken in two
The little town's a prison – the wall keeps them in
Bury my heart at Bethlehem
Where everyone's hidden from view
Forgotten and hidden from view

Garth Hewitt

When I visited Bethlehem in June and October of 2007 I was struck forcibly by the size of the wall and the way in which Bethlehem was hidden from view behind it. One of the most cynical comments must be the words written in huge letters on the wall by the Israeli Tourist Board: 'Peace be with you.' To lock people in a prison cell and wish them peace reveals an extraordinary level of cynicism. There is a security system at the gate of Bethlehem as there is at Ramallah and throughout the West Bank now. These are like security either at a prison or a more extreme version of what are at some airports; the Israelis call them 'terminals'. The only people who can go through these are people who have visas or permits to travel or, of course, international visitors. Palestinians mostly do not get permits to travel or visas, and those who do can find that these are not respected at the apparently arbitrary whim of the Israeli Defence Force (IDF) soldiers. For example, when I was there towards the end of September and beginning of October 2007, going through the security system, they made the man in front of me strip down to his underwear. The young man working for the IDF who made him do this did not even bother to come out of his glass cubicle.

There are daily humiliations. A woman was recently made to strip at the terminal security. The Israelis know this is unacceptable in Palestinian culture and they do it to humiliate people. I felt completely shocked when I saw it happening.

As well as this, a day or two later the feast of Succoth started, and instantly the whole of the Bethlehem area was closed down. (It may have been the whole of the West Bank but I only experienced it in Bethlehem.) So Wisam, our tour guide who was going to get my wife and other friends from the airport, came with his permit to do this on the second day of the feast and they simply turned him away. Bethlehem was closed down for all Palestinians during the time of the feast. It is quite shocking to think that one religion's feast can be used as a time of oppression against another group of people. It also continues to make life impossible for the Palestinians. If they have to meet a tour group then they cannot do it and they become unreliable and they lose the work.

Goodbye to Rachel's Tomb

Another example of the use of religion to oppress is Rachel's Tomb. Rachel's Tomb in Bethlehem has been well known to all three of the faiths for generations. It is a shrine that remembers that here in Bethlehem, Rachel died giving birth to Benjamin. This site, holy in some sense to the three faiths, includes a mosque and Muslim graveyard as well as being seen as very holy to Jewish people – there is a synagogue here, and it is respected by Christians. Between 1948 and 1967 it was protected by the Islamic Waqf and was open for Jewish worshippers. Now it has the wall completely surrounding it so it is impossible for either Muslims or Christians from Bethlehem to even get to the tomb. It has become part of Jerusalem, that is, a whole area of Bethlehem has been taken. Bishara Awad in

2006 took me to meet the last shopkeeper in the section of shops in the immediate vicinity of Rachel's Tomb. Seven of the shopkeepers had left, but one was still there. He was Charlie Khalil Judeh Musallem – he was selling sandwiches and groceries. When we met him, he wept because his trade was about to disappear. He said, 'Now I have no hope but God.'

When I went back in 2007, I asked Bishara about him and he said, 'Yes, they took him out and they closed the wall. When he said, "How can I run my business?" they said, "You can go round," but of course, he is not allowed out through the gate at Bethlehem. They said, "Apply for a permit," so he did. Of course, he has not got a permit, so his business has been taken.' So a holy site has been used to deprive people of their businesses. It has also been used to assert one religion over others. I tried to get in there this year and could not. I was told that if you go to a settlement, there is a bus that runs down for some people to visit. If that is the case, it is only accessible for Israelis and international visitors. Rabbi Jeremy Milgrom is particularly upset about the use of Rachel's Tomb in this way. He points out that a Muslim friend of his – Omar – from a refugee camp in Bethlehem says that the Muslims call the tomb of Rachel, 'Our mother' – this was their shorthand for the tomb. Jeremy said:

> Today Rachel's Tomb has been turned into a fortress – it is a monument to our insecurity, to our inability to recognize the Palestinians would respect Jewish yearnings and worship and attachment to a holy site. We feel there is a scarcity of blessing but I feel there's sufficient blessing for everybody.

The voices of Bethlehem which are reflected in the interviews in this book show something of how people are feeling, the degree of desperation at the loss of freedom of movement, freedom of worship, the loss of their economy, their fuel, the taking of the water, the taking of land and houses, the taking of green spaces. There is nowhere for the children to play in Bethlehem or Beit Sahour. The mayor of Beit Sahour took us to an area which used to be an army base, which they are trying to develop as a playground. They are longing for the children to have a place where they can play and climb and explore. When Wisam Salsaa came over to Britain in August 2007 and saw playgrounds all over the place, he felt anger that they have to be working so hard to get one such place for the children in their community when this is a natural right all around the world. Why must his children suffer when others have such a natural freedom?

Every aspect of human rights has been removed, and the depth of trauma in the community is now almost impossible to cope with. Wi'am Conflict Resolution Centre, which Amos partners in Bethlehem, has to address the rising level of trauma in the community. Zoughbi Zoughbi, the director, has taken me to see some of the *sulha* (reconciliation process) and reconciliation work being done. Because of the stress caused by the imprisonment and siege, it is breeding domestic violence and tension between families. So, along with his workers and volunteers, he tries to resolve these conflicts, and the community are very grateful. But he also points out that about 90 per cent of the children are traumatized, and the legacy of all this is very frightening. Consequently, it is not surprising that many families are leaving.

Christian families are leaving

A third of the Christian families have now left. As one friend of mine says, 'My father's generation suffered. My generation has suffered. I do not want my children to suffer. I want to get out.' Consequently, if it is possible to get out, many are trying to do this. Many Christians have links in the West, and so have been applying for visas. At the same time now, many middle-class Muslims are also trying to get out. Key people who should be helping to build the society for the future are leaving. It is also true that many liberal Jewish people are leaving as well. That these groups of people who would be key players in their own societies are going does not bode well for the future of this land.

A friend of mine decided he would leave. He had been imprisoned by the Israelis during the first intifada when he was 14 and tortured; when he came out of prison he was someone committed to non-violence and passionately committed to Palestine. But after he married and they had their first child, one night the Israeli army came into a building right next to theirs, shot someone, and threw them off the top of the roof. In all the shootings and explosions that occurred in this incident, as he clutched his daughter and protected her, he thought, 'I can no longer stay here with all of this.' He comes from Beit Sahour ('the shepherds' fields' area), and faithfully for centuries the Christian community here have witnessed to the gospel message and have also witnessed to non-violence.

One time I was asked to sing at the 'Cucumber Festival' in Beit Sahour. It was a most remarkable event. The main town centre was blocked off and dancers, poets and singers came from the local community and refugee camps. I did my singing and looked out across hundreds of people. As I wandered around watching it all and eating an unnaturally large number of cucumbers, I was invited into someone's house to drink coffee. Staring out of the doorway at all that was going on, I thought I had gone through some Narnian wardrobe and arrived in this extraordinary Christian town with its art and creativity, and I was observing this forgotten community of whom most of the world are totally unaware.

One of the richest experiences is to go inside the wall and visit Bethlehem, Beit Jala and Beit Sahour. But travel wherever you can in the West Bank. Go to Hebron and see what is happening there. Chat with the Christian Peacemaker teams and get them to show you around and talk about the pressure they are experiencing from the most heavily armed Israeli settlers. You will experience both the wonderful joy of such a lovely community but also the pain when the gun is harnessed to the Bible and used to oppress people.

Days in the desert with Wisam Salsaa and friends

One of the most memorable days of my visit in May was when I went down to the Judaean desert with Wisam, Ayman (Wisam's cousin) and Shadi, a singer from Dheisheh refugee camp. We drove in a jeep out through a village called Ubeidiyia, which had built up between the fourth and sixth centuries with people who came to support family members who were monks living in the Judaean desert. During this time, thousands were living inside cells or in caves in the desert. At the time of the Sassanian (Persian) invasion in 614 there were 10,000 monks living in the desert. We went to the hilltop next to Mar Saba monastery and sat down and looked over the valley and some of the caves. The valley is the Kidron Valley. We visited the monastery and spent some time talking to one of the monks. Later we sat on the rocks overlooking the monastery and the valley. Shadi sang a song called 'The last moon', and then we talked about it. Wisam said:

> It is a song that talks about 'in the night of the eclipse', or in a very dark night, there is no moon, and the beast is coming, and if we do not kill the dragon or the beast, this

17

will be our last moon. It is a very old song the people sang on different occasions warning each other about a threat coming from outside. We have a saying in Arabic, I have heard it since I was a baby: 'Nothing that comes from the West pleases your heart.' So that everything that comes from the West is bad. People always felt the danger coming from the West, from occupiers, from the Turks, for example, later from the British mandate, the Jewish creation of a new state in 1948 and then the *Naksa* (disappointment) in 1967.

(1947–1948 was called *Nakba* which means 'catastrophe'. The later defeat in 1967 was a further disappointment or *Naksa*.)

It was such a moving, quiet and inspiring time that the four of us went back to the desert in October taking Johnny, another friend of Wisam, and also Gill, my wife, and Sue and Simon Plater of Amos Trust. We went and sat in the same place. You can see why people would go there to get away from the few square miles of the Bethlehem area. It is a place to be reminded of the bigger world. It is a very beautiful and awesome place. Somehow you can feel that unjust regimes come and go but the world carries on. It is a place that strengthens spirituality and puts the world in perspective.

A day or two later Wisam said:

I was really shocked yesterday. I thought the desert that we went to would be connected to Bethlehem in one way or another, but it does not seem so because there is a bypass road completing the fence around Bethlehem. This will cut the desert off from us. So even the desert, even our desert – the beautiful desert – will be cut off from us. The desert for us is a place where we go and relax because there is no other place to go as you can see. It is over-crowded over here and there is no place to relax, to have some silence. I am really shocked – they are actually taking the desert.

Talking to him as I wrote this I checked if they were cut off from the desert. 'Yes,' he said, 'settlers are now driving through that road, and it has many watch towers to protect them.'

3

The fascinating story of Tawfiq Salsaa's walled nativity

They've cancelled Christmas (The wall must fall)
They've cancelled Christmas in Bethlehem
They've cancelled peace in Bethlehem
In a land once known as holy the gun is in control
They've cancelled Christmas in Bethlehem

They've cancelled freedom in Bethlehem
They've cancelled hope in Bethlehem
They've locked the little town behind a ghetto wall
They've cancelled Christmas in Bethlehem

Though angels are singing – they're trapped behind the wall
Yet angels keep singing down in Beit Sahour
And if our Christmas songs and prayers are not to be
in vain
We must pull down that prison wall that's strangling
Bethlehem

The wall must fall – the wall must fall
If peace on earth is to come
The wall must fall

They've cancelled wise men in Bethlehem
They've cancelled shepherds in Bethlehem

Tawfiq Salsaa's walled nativity

They've stopped the wise men at the checkpoint and the
shepherds can't leave home
They're under curfew in Bethlehem

Though angels are singing . . .

The wall must fall – the wall must fall
If peace on earth is to come
The wall must fall . . .

They've cancelled Christmas in Bethlehem
Garth Hewitt

Tawfiq Salsaa has been working in olive wood for many years.
He sits and carves it in his little workshop along with others
who are working with him. At Amos Trust for the last few years
we have been selling his olive-wood items and those made by
others from his community to raise support for Beit Sahour
and the local neighbourhood. Because tourism has largely disappeared, we have been trying to support the work they have
traditionally done until tourists comes back. Tawfiq Salsaa
made a very beautiful nativity set which had a separation wall
across it with the wise men unable to get through to visit the
holy family. Over in Britain, it would have been sold at around
£50, and it was a beautiful set that was ideal for churches.

He had been thinking about the flight to Egypt: how would
the holy family get through to Egypt today? They would not
be able to; they would be caught inside Bethlehem. He was
reflecting the lack of movement and opportunity. One of
the lovely aspects of his nativity is that the wall is removable.
In other words, when the wall comes down, you can remove
the wall from your nativity set. However, at the same time,
Chris Rose at Amos suggested that he made a smaller version
which people could put on their tables in their homes to

remind them of the Bethlehem community and the struggle for justice. So they made a version that was sold at around £12.

At Amos, we issued a press release about this because we felt that people would be interested to know that it was available, and we were quite overwhelmed at the response. Some of the articles were very well and sensitively written. Reuters Jerusalem went and interviewed Tawfiq and photographed him and put a beautiful article together, and so the walled nativity was shown in context. The Ship of Fools website put together twelve kitsch items of Christmas and added the walled nativity as the thirteenth to show it as an aspect of protest or to make people think about Christmas and the situation in Bethlehem. This is a website viewed by huge numbers of people around the world, so it raised even more publicity. Anyone who knows Amos knows the way we work with partners and with those who are Christian, Jew or Muslim, in other words, those of all faiths or none, and that we are committed to both Palestine and Israel. But as the news spread around the world (quite literally), two things happened. First, we had an overwhelming response from people wanting to order the walled nativity, which we certainly could not meet. Second, we received a lot of emails that seemed to have been co-ordinated, and which were basically abusive. They were unaware of Amos in terms of who we work with, but also they seemed to have no sense of what was happening in Bethlehem or who had made the nativity. Some even called it anti-Semitic, ironically, as it is a nativity set made by a Semitic person who, along with his community, is suffering deeply.

The ignorance of what is going on in Bethlehem was overwhelming in these critical emails we received. Also, there was an assumption that the wall had stopped suicide bombers and presumably an assumption that it was on the border because there appeared to be no knowledge that it was such a land grab and was such an imprisonment and siege of the community. There was, therefore, much more offence taken at Tawfiq Salsaa making his tiny little wall rather than the huge wall that is depriving so many of their human rights. (Incidentally, if the wall was built on the border, though many people may dislike it, it would not receive the criticism it is now receiving because it could be seen genuinely as to do with security rather than an imprisonment and a land grab.)

The most disturbing aspect, though, of the critical letters was the way a large number were not only abusive but racist and Islamaphobic. There was repeated vitriol about Muslims, Arabs and Palestinians and no sense of finding a way forward in terms of dialogue, justice and peacemaking. The lesson that we learned from this was the importance in all work about Palestine and Israel of asserting the equal humanity and the equal rights of all. The assumption that one group must win and must dominate and must take over the land, often in the name of God, is a tribal and primitive view and simply does not lead to the possibility of peace or good relationships. It would in the end only lead to conflict.

When I was interviewed by the *Jewish Chronicle*, it was the first time I heard that people were calling the nativity set anti-Semitic; I laughed when the journalist told me that because I was so surprised. He agreed that he did not think it was. He said, 'Surely it has nothing to do with Judaism.' But he said he would include some quotes from people who disagreed with him. It was interesting to read these quotes as they were all from Christian Zionists, one of whom was appalled that Christmas was used in this way, saying it should be 'about hope and unity'. 'Exactly', I thought. Let us give some hope to the Palestinians. Let us give some unity by taking down the wall and bringing a unity of opportunity to both Palestinian and Israeli. Surely that is the message of Christmas and there can be no road to peace with 10,000 prisoners in Israeli jails and the rest of Gaza and the West Bank caught behind the wall. Preserving the status quo by silence will only let injustice flourish. The demand for Tawfiq Salsaa's walled nativity still goes on, and you can order it from Amos Trust until the wall comes down!

4

Voices from Bethlehem (and about Bethlehem)

Candle of hope
Bethlehem house of bread
Womb of hope let all be fed

Voices sing as hope is born
A chance of peace for everyone
But refugees cry out tonight
Forgotten ones can't see the light

Bethlehem house of bread
Womb of hope let all be fed

There's a candle of hope in Bethlehem
Starting afresh in Bethlehem
The light is here through all the pain
So don't put out that fragile fame
Garth Hewitt

This chapter and the next two contain the heart of this book. They are the voices of 16 witnesses, some brief and some in much more detail. The voices raise issues, speak practically, prophetically, politically and theologically. They paint an extraordinary picture of life in Palestine and particularly in the Bethlehem area. Not all are voices from Bethlehem – some are from East Jerusalem, some from Galilee. They are ordinary people – good people – they are voices of humanity calling for justice; calling for the same human rights that we expect in Britain and Europe, that people expect in the United States and that people expect in Israel – no more but no less. It is time to listen. In this chapter seven witnesses speak.

Witness 1: Sawsan Zeidan
They have taken the view

My visit in May/June 2007 began with breakfast at the Jacir Palace hotel in Bethlehem – just a matter of yards from the wall. I was served by Sawsan Zeidan. She is 25 years old, qualified from Bethlehem University in hotel management, and is currently working as a waitress. She is a Christian – Lutheran on her mother's side and Greek Orthodox on her father's side. Her father died when she was five and two of her brothers left school to provide for the family – they are carpenters. She has three brothers and one sister.

Asking her about the situation she said:

> You have to keep hope because without this you will lose everything. You must have faith – faith that something will happen and faith in God.
>
> I would like to live a normal life with no wars and to have my rights to live here as a human being.
>
> Fighting does not resolve anything. When Israelis kill Palestinians then Palestinians respond; it is action and reaction.
>
> I reject violence as a way to solve problems.
>
> Every day I pass beside the wall – I live near it – I feel I am in a prison. You cannot see anything – they have taken the view and of course they have taken a lot of land.

The main thing is to stop the fighting and for us to blend together. I would like to see one society. One state is the solution because two states will not work. You have seen the map – how we are divided – you cannot consider that as a state.

I hear that they will take our family land. When the wall is finished we will not be able to visit our land.

Whoever comes here is shocked; the media in your country is trying to block things out from the viewers. They do not want them to see what is really going on in Palestine. They do not want to show violence against Palestinians, but they do show violence against Israelis. Why? I do not know – I am not a politician!

Witness 2: Zoughbi Zoughbi
Rebuild relationships: choose life and humanity

Zoughbi Zoughbi is the Director of Wi'am, which is a conflict resolution centre in Bethlehem and an Amos Trust partner. Zoughbi is the epitome of ecumenism. He was baptized Greek Orthodox, confirmed a Roman Catholic, but now goes to the Melkite church in Bethlehem, and if he was allowed to go to Jerusalem he says he would go to the Lutheran church there! He lives in a very ecumenical family and Wi'am has worked with all the churches.

Our hopes are destroyed by the wall

Currently in Bethlehem we have the feeling that we are in jail – a very small jail. It is smaller than the time when we met last and it has been getting smaller and smaller. Actually the whole country has become a walled jail. The wall is this 750-km snake surrounding not only the West Bank but enclosing every area and separating it from other areas. You feel not only in jail but also isolated and disconnected. You cannot visit your family in Jerusalem and it is very difficult to go from the south to the north in the West Bank.

I see the bleeding of my people – at least a hundred families have left the area and more young people are leaving. I do not think we have an accurate account of how many people are leaving.

So there is this imprisonment – the people are dispersed – our dreams are shattered, and our hopes are destroyed by the wall.

From grotto to ghetto

The wall is not for security, the wall is not for creating better conditions for the Israelis: the wall is the best mechanism of bureaucracy that Israel can use to confiscate more land. Bethlehem has moved from being the grotto to the ghetto. The city council [Zoughbi is on the city council] tried to have a playground and we planned to have it on the northern side. But the northern side has been confiscated, so we do not have any big spaces in which to have a playground or public spaces for the use of the people. So it triggers more domestic violence and deteriorating health conditions. There is more demoralization and there is more displaced anger and frustration, and I feel that is why it is important to be involved in the ministry of reconciliation. The problem is the Israeli government likes to have their cake and eat it; they are not yet ready to exchange land for peace and this really makes it impossible.

I feel the dawn will come

I feel the dawn will come; no matter how long is the darkness of the night and how ugly is the darkness, the dawn *will* come. *When* it will come is the issue and I feel the Israeli government will delay the inevitable.

I think the dawn will come by perseverance, by appealing to the wider community, by enticing the collective responsibility of the world community. The Palestinians need to continue their struggle non-violently for peace with justice. The pro-justice campaigners need to continue their preventative non-violence to get rid of the occupier.

Then the collective responsibility of prophetic voices and secular movements need to exert pressure on Israel to come to their senses and implement the UN resolutions.

I do not think this will happen through military confrontation – only through enticing the collective responsibility, and we saw the collective responsibility at work to end the apartheid regime in South Africa. The World Council of Churches played a key role, the prophetic voices of the Church there in South Africa played a role, the prophetic voice of the churches in Britain and other places worked well through disinvestment and through empowering the weak. We need a similar response. I call it the collective responsibility because it is the only mechanism for making Israel come to terms with the Security Council resolutions. In the meantime it feels it is a superpower; it has the only power here. When Israel is humble, I believe there will be a process to peace, but no process is going to be easy. I believe when the United States' aid for Israel becomes accountable, when it can be questioned, when the citizens of Israel and Palestine are treated equally, when there is disinvestment from any Israeli company that perpetuates the occupation, when there is pressure on multi-transglomerates from government levels, and from the people's level.

Bethlehem Speaks

Thoughts about British responsibility

I would like to say to the British Prime Minister: have more understanding of the Middle East, especially when we think of the history of British involvement in our cause. It is time to revise it; it is time to look in the mirror at what you have done to the Palestinians. I would like to invite him to see the Palestinians, to stay in their hotels and to have a tour around Bethlehem and other areas and to see what the wall is doing; to see the settlements, to make comparisons between the settlements and the Palestinian cities.

I would like to invite him to see and have a first-hand knowledge of all sides. I believe the British people generally like to deliver freedom. They do not like to occupy or to humiliate or enslave others. The British people seem more aware of what is going on and they like to be more involved in a different way than their government, so I would say: listen to the people. Then I hope that Britain will assume its responsibility in handling issues in a different way. We are not asking anyone to be a friend of the Palestinians, we do not want anyone to be pro-Palestinian, but to let justice be their lens in dealing with Palestinians and Israelis. I am not interested in creating another victim of any people; we are looking for empowering the way of the oppressed and bringing the powerful to their senses. This is where I hope the British officials will have a different perspective as a result of their visits, and as a result of their fact-finding missions.

Message to church leaders: you are the voice of justice

To church leaders I would say: listen to what our Lord is asking us to do. What does the Lord require from you?

To do justice, show mercy and walk humbly. I believe church leaders have this responsibility and that is why when I talk about the British officials, I am talking also about church leaders.

I am not interested in enhancing the victim mentality or the guilt in others, and that is why I call for the collective responsibility. The churches have a bigger responsibility because they are the voice of justice – it is time to be liberated from the guilt feeling that the Zionist movement and the state of Israel is perpetuating. It is time to be liberated and to look at issues from an inclusive point of view and not to be afraid to be called 'anti-Semitic'. Pro-justice Jewish groups must not be afraid if they are called 'self-hating Jews'. This responsibility will be asked in front of God, 'What were our actions?' – 'Did we do anything to stop the occupation?'

Our Lord has always reminded us that 'whatever you do to the least of my brothers, you are doing to me'. We are all brothers and sisters and this responsibility is carried on and I hope that the Church will not only have a prophetic voice but also will have meaningful dialogue with all governments and work for justice from an inclusive point of view.

I feel the churches did an excellent job in South Africa, but it is time for them to do it in the land of Christ and not to be 'anti' but 'pro' justice. We are living in the land of miracles – miracles could happen – the peace message can start again. It is not impossible because Archbishop Tutu and other bishops who have been involved in the ending of apartheid had that experience. As Martin Luther King says, 'any injustice anywhere is injustice everywhere', and if we focus on and talk about every human being as being created in the image of God it will liberate us.

31

Farewell to the forgotten faithful?

I do not think that we will disappear. It is not by chance we were born here. I feel our people have been here for two thousand years and will continue. Many times our ancestors have lived through such bleak situations and they have survived; I think the Church is alive and its witness is strong and it will continue. Maybe this is the worst time for our forgotten faithful, but I think the community will stay if, again and only if, we are able to address the needs of this community.

Jesus is alive in many leaders here and there are many prophetic voices. The wolves sometimes appear to be stronger but also the faithful are strong too. And we are strengthened by the visits of groups from around the world. The needs are big and the challenges are great but hope is alive.

We should respect the results of democracy

I respect the different political groups that live in this area. I differ with some of them but if we talk about democracy, we should respect the results of democracy, not to take what we want and boycott the other. Secondly, I hope the responsibility also of those elected from Hamas will meet the challenge that they are not running a small party, but they are running a government responsible for the community, and also under the responsibility of the world community. So they should meet the needs of the local, regional and international communities and help the Palestinians to figure out their own business, and how to build a society based on accountability. Without a political settlement, this land will witness more conflicts. This is the best time for a relationship to be reconstructed because all parties are exhausted and are looking for a better relationship.

'Human security' is a better term than 'peace'

I believe we need to look for a different terminology than the word 'peace' because it is exhausted; it is misused and it is overused. I suggest 'human security' as a term. We are looking for our human security and each others' human security. I also use the word 'justice', which is the backbone of human security. We need to look at human security from an inclusive point of view and from a justice point of view.

Every day there is a peace proposal, a peace process, a peace something, and here it is used sometimes to justify the policies of the state of Israel. We need to think outside the box, to think more creatively. Now when you say there is another peace process going to happen, automatically people lose confidence in it.

I focus more on the term 'justice' from a more inclusive point of view. To start again to humanize each other is very important. We have demonized each other to the point that we legitimize the killing of each other; we need to rediscover the humanity in each other, we need to go on a structural journey, to go back to the roots of our monotheistic spirituality and be reminded that we are created in the image of God and every human life is holy.

This is a very important message – because otherwise there will be no peace and there will be no restoration of relationships.

Hope is a form of non-violence

All of it is a call for hope, and for me hope is a form of non-violence: it is the energizer, it is the catalyst, it is the faith. But also, we should be reminded when we talk about hope that there is a risk and a promise to it. For me, hope that is not risking is not hope, and hope that is not promising is not hope. We would like to see as a part of the promise hope that will create more life rather than death. So it is a choice for life, it is a choice for humanity and a choice for creating a different energy in the Middle East.

Sooner or later the wall *will* fall, not only the physical wall, but the wall of separation, the wall of grudges.

Let us learn from history. We should be open to tell our stories, to work with others and to put an end to the cycle of violence, so that the victims of yesterday will not be the perpetrators of tomorrow's suffering. The only way to break the cycle of violence is through justice.

Witness 3: Mitri Raheb
Bethlehem: the soul of Palestine

Dr Mitri Raheb is senior pastor at Christmas Lutheran Church and President of Al-Diyar, which is a consortium of several church-related organizations in Bethlehem including the international culture and conference centre of Bethlehem, the Dar al-Kalima College focusing on art, music, communication and media, and a health and wellness centre.

Bethlehem a big open-air prison

The little town of Bethlehem has been turned into a big open-air prison surrounded by nine-metre high walls with three gates. One is finished, one is almost finished, and a third is under construction, and guess who will have keys to those gates? The Israeli military.

34

So what does this mean for people, economically for example, since Bethlehem depends on tourism? Imagine if Israel would say, 'We will close up today so no tourists can enter Bethlehem.' Now people think that this is not likely to happen, but I question that assumption because this has already been the case in Gaza for five years. Seventy per cent of the economy of Bethlehem depends on tourism, so if Israel stops tourists from entering Bethlehem, the city will die.

The city cannot expand and water and land is taken

If you look exactly where the wall is put you will see that it is in the backyard of the last home in town, which really means that the city cannot expand horizontally. We cannot build new neighbourhoods; we cannot have new suburbs, and a city that cannot expand will die. But that also means that if you look carefully, you will see that the wall is built in such a way that all the green areas of the land of Bethlehem are trapped on the other side of the wall.

Around 1,835 Palestinian Christian families have land and olive groves on the other side of the wall. This means that they cannot access their olive trees any more.

This year they cannot pick olives there because they need a permit to go and pick olives. Think of our children five years from now: there will be no green area left in Bethlehem, and imagine what this means if your children growing up in our city do not know how spring looks or what it smells like.

With that comes the psychological effect of the wall because people feel somehow they are getting suffocated – they cannot breathe. And so depression is a major issue.

Also, the wall is built in such a way that four major aquifers are placed on the other side. So basically our land, our water resources, our tourist attractions are all getting stolen by the Israeli military from the Bethlehem-ites. The Bethlehem region during Jordanian rule went all the way to the Dead Sea. So basically Israel has 87 per cent of the area of Bethlehem under its control.

Optimism and hope

I like to distinguish between optimism and hope, so if you ask me, 'Are you optimistic?' I tell you 'No, not at all'. Because what I see is that we are heading with full force towards an apartheid system. This is, I think, why President Carter in his latest book has called it *Palestine: Peace or Apartheid*. He is saying Israel has to choose now – not tomorrow, but now – either they want peace or apartheid. If they do not choose peace within the current year, then basically they have opted for an apartheid system. This is what I am seeing getting implemented.

I think for the coming two generations Israel and the Palestinians will be living under such an apartheid system. So there is no reason for optimism – on the contrary.

This, however, does not mean that I am not hopeful, because for me hope is something different to optimism. Optimism is thinking that tomorrow is going to be better. But if you live here and you are realistic you know tomorrow is not going to be better, besides you can read the signs on the wall. But hope is not something we see. Hope is something we do. And this is why here in our work we see the need to create 'facts on the ground'. Israel is creating destructive 'facts on the ground'; we have to create constructive facts on the ground. Everything else is just a waste of time. So we do not like to participate in what I call 'peace-talking events' – when people meet and talk about peace and so on. We need peacemakers, people who really create facts. And this is why we are busy building institutions, one institution after the other, hiring young Palestinian Christians but also Muslims, and providing a vision for the future. So basically what we are doing here is instead of telling the people how Palestine could look in the future, we are showing them today the potential of Palestine and we are giving them a foretaste of what is to come.

The waste of peace-talking

I went recently to visit a church member for his eighty-fifth birthday. I asked him, 'How many high-level delegations did you see during your lifespan coming here to solve the conflict?' Almost every day we have high-level delegations. Condoleezza Rice alone came to Israel/Palestine around fourteen times, and she will come again next week. They come and go, they come and go, they come and go, so there is plenty of peace-talking but you do not feel anything on the ground.

The solution is easy

What a waste of resources and what a waste of time and what a waste of energy just to keep managing the conflict rather than solving it. The problem here is that the solution is very easy. It is not that people have to reinvent the wheel. It is very easy but there is no will on the Israeli side and the international community is cowardly and they cannot speak justice to the Israelis.

The real city of Bethlehem, Palestine

It is important to know that first of all Bethlehem is a real city, that this city is located in Palestine. Many people think Bethlehem is in Israel.

People also need to know that in Bethlehem today we have the largest concentration of Christians throughout the West Bank and Gaza – over 50 per cent of all Christians living in the West Bank and Gaza live in Bethlehem. This means that if Christianity disappeared from Bethlehem it would mean that it has disappeared from everywhere else. But also I think it is important for groups or churches, when they think of Bethlehem, not to think only of what God did two thousand years ago here, but to see what God is doing here and now.

'Come, let us go to Bethlehem and see the facts on the ground'

I think the Christmas story already gives us some hints as to how you can support us. For example, when the angel appeared to the shepherds in the fields, they looked at each other and said, 'Come, let us go to Bethlehem and see this thing that the Lord has proclaimed to us.' In another translation it reads something like, 'Come, let us go to Bethlehem and see the facts on the ground.' So in that sense, I think coming here, staying in Bethlehem, spending money here, is something very important. Because 98 per cent of the tourism benefits only Israel and just 2 per cent really benefits the Palestinians. So tourism is one major obstacle towards economic justice. Second, the three magi brought with them gifts, and it is important also that groups who come here bring their gifts. I am not talking about money necessarily; I am talking about their skills, their energy, their ideas, but also that they do something very concrete here, because Christmas is not about a God who remains so far away from us. It is about God who became incarnate and one of us, and this is why our work has to be very much incarnational.

Bethlehem – the soul of Palestine

Bethlehem is the second most affected city by the wall after Qalqilya (the worst). This is for several reasons. One reason is that Bethlehem is a fertile area. Another reason is that Bethlehem symbolizes the soul of Palestine and they really want to kill the soul. It was not by chance that Jesus said, 'Fear those who kill the soul, not only those who kill the body'. But also I think Israel would like to see the Palestinian Christians disappear from the horizon because if they disappear then this conflict becomes very much Muslims versus Jews. In such a conflict it is clear where the world will stand – with Israel. So the Palestinian Christians are a stumbling block in those calculations.

Even theology has been very much influenced by some racist ideologies like Zionism, and many people are not aware that there are Palestinian Christians. They do not know what to do with us. We are a stumbling block. But if you look carefully, we can see that most probably I have more Jewish blood in me than those imported from Russia or from Ethiopia and so on. But who cares in the end? It is about politics and less about theology.

Witness 4: Wisam Salsaa
No freedom, no place to walk, no relaxation, nothing but tension

Wisam Salsaa is a Palestinian tour guide from Beit Sahour (the Shepherds' Fields). Married to Rasha, they have two children, Leah Ann and Sarah – my godchildren! His father is Tawfiq Salsaa who made the walled nativity.

I am very angry

I am very angry, I do not like it, I hate the wall, I hate the settlements; I think that we no longer have any chance for the future in this prison because, as you see, Bethlehem is completely closed.

I think that the situation will get worse and worse, because even though they talk about peace and they talk about solutions, look what's happening on the ground.

How can we live in peace if there is a wall going around us and there are even settlements behind these walls and they are still building settlements? So we are talking about peace today and the bulldozers are taking more land and pulling up trees around here and making something permanent on the ground. That means that we'll never have peace. At least, where I live, we'll never have peace.

Peace for me is freedom.

Peace for me means justice.

Peace does not simply mean smiling and saying 'Hello' to the Israelis. This is not peace. I do not think the future will be good over here unless something happens, and I do not see anything happening soon.

Message to the British Prime

I would like to tell the British Prime Minister, 'Be a man. Don't be afraid of the Americans. Go and see the truth and do what you should do. As a human, as a Christian, as a Prime Minister you must be brave. We need a brave person to take the initiative and do something against injustice.'

Message to the churches

For many years, we are giving the same message to the churches – help the locals, help the Christians, keep the 'living stones here'. I would say this year that my message would be different. I would tell them, let's try to celebrate without Christians in Bethlehem. Help us to get out from here. Maybe they would do that.

Do something – either help us to stay or help us to get out, but please help. Please do something. We need the story to be told. We need people lobbying on our behalf. Put pressure on your government to take a step towards justice in Palestine/Israel. This would be very effective.

Support projects, help people to survive, support schools, scholarships, sick people and hospitals. At least let people have their basic needs so they can keep their dignity. Of course it is very important for people to come here. The best way is for people to see with their own eyes what is going on. It is more important than anything else.

People here are very peaceful people.

People want to live.

People want to love.

People want to dream.

That's why I'm still here because people are good.

Go to the villages. Go to the refugee camps. You feel at home. You feel the warmth. This is something that you do not always see anywhere else.

Witness 5: Alex Awad
The moral obligation to stand with justice

Alex Awad is pastor of the East Jerusalem Baptist Church and the Dean of Students at Bethlehem Bible College. He is also one of the mission representatives of the United Methodist Church in Palestine. Alex's church is an international, interdenominational congregation in East Jerusalem. It is a small congregation with 25 to 30 people. People in Bethlehem and Ramallah who used to come are no longer able to get there, so the congregation now is mainly internationals who live in Jerusalem. He was born in Jerusalem two years before the 1948 Arab–Israeli war.

A citizen of Palestine before creation of the state of Israel

I do not have any passport other than an American passport. I do not have even an Israeli or a Palestinian passport. I lost the right of citizenship in this country when I went to study abroad. I went first to Europe for my biblical education, then I continued in the United States. Then through the process of studying abroad I could not keep up with all the Israeli regulations that they put on Palestinians who wanted to keep up their residency and so I lost the right of residency. When I came back to my country, the Israelis told me I am no longer a citizen. So right now I am equal to any other clergyman or -woman who has a tourist visa or a permanent visa. The permanent visa is an A-3 visa and the Israelis give it to clergy personnel, so my wife and I are like missionaries from Germany or New Zealand. We have to stay in line to get a visa to live in this country, even though I was born here.

I was a citizen of Palestine before the creation of the state of Israel. I tried to raise this with with the Israeli Ministry of Interior and Ministry of Foreign Affairs, but for seven years I had to fight from outside the country because they would not permit me to be in the country even though I had a church here that wanted me and I had a Bible college that wanted me.

For seven years the Israelis denied me the right of access to the country of my birth. The ban stopped in 1993 with the signing of the Oslo Agreement. I took advantage of the Oslo Agreement and I came to the country and I was not deported. So right now I use my American naturalization, my citizenship, to take advantage of living in this country. Otherwise I could not continue my ministry here.

I live outside the wall in a village right across from Tantur. I commute to Bethlehem Bible College almost every day. My disadvantage, the fact that I do not have Palestinian papers, is giving me an advantage over my fellow brothers and sisters in Palestine because with my American passport and no Palestinian papers I can go in and out of the checkpoint just like any other foreigner. But here is the catch: if the Israelis decide at any time that I am *persona non grata*, they can kick me out of the country. So as long as I am in their good graces, I am allowed to stay.

I was born in a neighbourhood of Jerusalem very close to the New Gate, right behind Notre Dame. We lived there until 1948, and in 1948 the war took place and we became refugees after my father was killed in the war, not as a soldier but as a civilian. So my mother took the seven children and we fled to East Jerusalem, and we lived in East Jerusalem as refugees.

The occupation is no secret any more

There are important voices in the world speaking out against injustices and this gives me hope. About a year ago, former President Jimmy Carter came up with his book focusing on this issue. Even Tony Blair coming, hopefully with good intentions, and trying to broker peace between Israelis and Palestinians, is good. So there is a new focus and an uncovering of the filth of occupation, of the ugliness and the injustice and the brutality of Israeli occupation of the Palestinian people. It is not secret any more and the people of the world know about it, and therefore many hearts are changing especially in Europe and hopefully eventually in the United States.

The ghettos of Palestine

The wall is turning Palestinian towns and villages into isolated ghettos; some more and some less. Bethany, for instance, has become like an oasis with walls all around it, and with just one road going out of it to the West Bank, and even that road can be blocked at any time by Israelis. So people in Bethany have been weaned from their source of income. About 90–95 per cent used to work in Jerusalem. Bethany is like the sleeping community of the city of Jerusalem, and it is like cutting a suburb of a city off from its mother, from its centre. So the people in Bethany are frustrated. They cannot go to Jerusalem, which is only about three to four kilometres away. They cannot resume their work. They cannot get out of Bethany without a permit. A woman who cleans our church comes from Bethany. She applied for a permit through our church. I had to sign the letter, and we sent the letter again and again and again, and we tried to call – it is such a painful ordeal to try to get these permits. All our efforts failed. She said, 'Alex, I have a friend in the United States. Maybe I can get him to do something.' I said, 'By all means. Anything. Anything.' She called some guy in Michigan. He called the Israeli authorities. She was able to get a permit. Just to go and clean our church. Why does it have to come that way? Why do we have to go to a person in America to do this for us? Why can't the Israelis say, 'This is a peaceful woman who just wants to go to East Jerusalem, not even West Jerusalem, to simply clean up a church.'

It is the weaning off of the Palestinian people from Jerusalem. It is telling the Palestinian Muslims and Christians, Jerusalem does not belong to you any more. Forget about Jerusalem. Get used to living without Jerusalem.

Christians can come as long as they can be nice tourists. They can come, pay their dues, and go, but Christians cannot inhabit Jerusalem. Muslims cannot inhabit Jerusalem. They are turning Jerusalem into a Jewish entity where Muslims and Christians will not have a place to stay or a place to reside.

Tragedy after tragedy after tragedy

Bethany is a great tragedy. It is only three kilometres away from Jerusalem – the people of Bethany are just a step away from their brothers and sisters in East Jerusalem and yet they cannot get to them. They are doing this to us also in Bethlehem to cut us off from Jerusalem. This is separating not only people from their place of labour where they can make a living but also dividing families from families. A mother can be living on one side of the wall and her daughter can be living on the other side of the wall and those who are living on the inside of the wall cannot visit those on the outside of the wall. To have to ask for a permit to visit your family is absurd. You have to have a 'legitimate' reason to visit your mum or your dad or your grandpa – it is absurd, so it does not happen.

You cannot say my sister is having a baby in Jerusalem, I need to go and see her – all of these human needs are considered insignificant now.

So the wall has caused tragedy after tragedy after tragedy.

Getting a permit is harder than picking the olives

All the farmers who have land outside the wall cannot go and till their land, they cannot pick the olives. You have

45

to have a permit to go and pick olives, but getting a permit is harder than picking the olives, and picking the olives is hard! That is what we are facing every day. Now some people in Bethlehem have totally given up; because for them, they can go to Cairo, Egypt, over the bridge, or they can go to Germany or to the United States, more easily than going to Jerusalem which is less than ten kilometres away.

So the Israelis are creating these ghettos where Palestinians are limited to the land within the wall, which is only about 12–15 per cent of historic Palestine. This means Israel now has access to over 85 per cent of historic Palestine. In 60 years Palestinians have lost over 85 per cent of their historic homeland. That is tragic for any nation. You do not have to be an Arab or a Palestinian to realize this. It does not matter whether you are Muslim or Christian, for any people within 60 years to lose over 85 per cent of their national territory is really tragic, and that is what the Christians in Europe need to know. This is where the Church needs to say there is something wrong going on. Look at the map. Look at what is left for the Palestinians, instead of looking at the slogans of the Israelis and their crocodile tears about wanting peace.

The hard road to peace

There are segments of the Israeli society who want peace. There are many Israelis who are not aware of the dreams of their politicians who do want peace. Many Israelis assume that 100 per cent of the problem is with the Palestinians because they do not know what is going on on the ground. They do not know the issues. They do not know what we are experiencing from day to day. They do not know about the land confiscation; they do not know about the house demolitions. All they know about is what the Israelis tell them in the media about Palestinian terror and militancy, and they think the Palestinians are the obstacle to peace because they do all the ugly stuff, not knowing all that is being done here by Israeli troops. I may be naive, but it is hard to think that any human would not want peace. But if you study the history of Israeli governments, you can say historically the Israeli political system did not want peace. And why did they not want peace? Because they had a programme and they had to finish their programme. Their programme is to Judaize as much of the West Bank and of Jerusalem as possible. Once they achieve their goal of putting their hand on as much of Palestine as they possibly could, then they are going to say, now we want peace.

It is up to the Palestinians if they are willing to accept 10–15 per cent of historic Palestine as their future home-land. If that is all Israel is going to offer the Palestinians, I do not expect peace. This is where we need the Church, where we need the United Nations, where we need the international community to convince Israel that if you want peace, live and let live. Give the Palestinians most of the West Bank and the Gaza Strip and be satisfied with 78 or 80 per cent of historic Palestine. Palestinians are asking only for 20 or 22 per cent, so if the Israelis would give about 20 per cent, I think the Palestinians would sign the peace agreement tomorrow. But now, the Israelis are giving the Palestinians between 12 and 15 per cent. But, I think the Israelis should be willing to give 20–22 per cent (which is the West Bank and the Gaza Strip). If they do not give that land, they should substitute land from the Negev or somewhere else – an inch for an inch. You see with Barak it failed because Barak said Palestinians should take one inch for every ten inches that the Israelis would have taken from the West Bank. That would not work. That was arrogant. This is why Yasser Arafat objected and this is why they demonized him, and blamed him for the failure of the Camp David accords in 2000. However, I do think there are a good number of Israelis who are willing to give up the West Bank and the Gaza Strip for a political solution, but it is the hard-line Zionists in the United States and the hard-line Zionists in Israel who are the ones who want to get as much of Palestine as possible before there is a peace agreement. They do not understand that if they want all of that, it will be really hard to come to a peace agreement.

Gaza and Hamas

I feel very sad for the people of Gaza most of all. They do not deserve all this punishment. Hamas is not as evil as Israel is trying to project it to the world. They are Islamic, they are fundamentalist, but we have our Christian fundamentalists and the Jewish people have their fundamentalists. They do not all have horns and they are not all terrorists! When Yasser Arafat was President of the Palestinian people, the Israelis called him a terrorist. When he was out of the way we have Mahmoud Abbas. Mahmoud Abbas is a kind man. He wanted to make peace. But the Israelis wanted to find a reason why they cannot make peace so they did not give Abbas anything. He wanted a release of prisoners; they would not give him that.

He wanted to talk with them on the disengagement from Gaza; they did not want to talk with him. They totally marginalized him. When you marginalize him then he cannot deliver for his people. So his people are going to forget about him and that turned the Palestinians to Hamas. It was a vote of defiance. It is not that Palestinians are saying, 'We are Islamic fundamentalists, that is why we vote for Hamas.' It is not because Palestinians are saying, 'We want to destroy the state of Israel and that is why we are voting for Hamas.' Absolutely not.

It is a vote of defiance against the corruption in the PLO.

It is a vote of defiance against the Israeli politics of ignoring the Palestinian Authority and the peaceful dialogue.

It is a vote of defiance against full US support for Sharon and his evil. Also it is the Palestinians saying, instead of supporting the team that are stealing our money, why don't we support the team that is helping the poor, which is Hamas?

So for all these four reasons Palestinians voted for Hamas.

Now once Hamas was voted for, I as a Christian was disappointed because I do not want a militant Islamic group to be head of my government, but the western world made another mistake. Instead of giving Hamas time to fail, they start working for the failure of Hamas. And when you do that, it is like pouring water over fire – you make it go wild.

They should have accepted the democratic vote. They should have let it work, and Hamas would either die by itself or Hamas would get out of its valley and onto the summit and at the summit it will reform. If they had allowed Hamas leaders to talk to the French or to the Italians or the Germans or the United Nations, usually those people get rehabilitated and they would get reformed, and they would change their stance on Israel and other issues.

But with George Bush and the Israeli hardliners they did not get a chance, and against international law the Israelis started taking elected officials and putting them in jail. This is ridiculous. So now Hamas becomes the victim and everybody with Palestine wants to support the victim, because the victim is the one who is standing against the United States and against Israel. They see the President (Abbas) is trying to shake hands with the Americans and the Israelis but his hand is always an empty hand because they do not put anything in it. It is really very, very sad.

Our Christian mandate

We have a moral obligation to stand with justice.

We have a moral obligation to stand with what is right. This is even more important than a prophecy in the book of Ezekiel or a statement that came six thousand years ago in the book of Joshua.

Our Christian mandate is to show the love of God to the world, and to seek justice for everybody. So my advice to Christian leaders in the UK and anywhere else in the world is, first, come and see what is happening. Come and see the reality. Come and see the wall. Come and see how many Christian families have lost lands that have been with them for hundreds of years. Come and see the daily pain of both the Christian and also of the Muslim community. Come and see how much land the Palestinians have lost. Come and see who is throwing who where. It is not the Palestinians who are throwing the Israelis into the sea. It is the other way around. Come and see and then act to try to do what is just and acceptable. And peace is not against the will of God. Peace is in harmony with God's will. Anyone who says peace is the work of the devil or the Antichrist does not know the nature of Christ and the nature of the New Testament. So this is my advice. Come and see and then advocate. Do not wait for the secular people to defend justice and do not wait for Muslim leaders around the world to defend justice. I would rather have seen the Archbishop of Canterbury speak about the rights of the Palestinian people than Ahmadinejad of Iran.

We Christians, we need to take a stand for truth and justice and not leave it for atheists or for the secular people or for people of other religions because this is the mandate that Christ has given to us.

Witness 6: Fuad Dagher
We have to be a prophetic voice despite the hopeless situation

Fuad Dagher is Vicar of St Paul's Church, Shefa'Amr, Galilee. Married to Hanna with two children, he has been known to me since he was in the youth group at Christ Church, Nazareth. He is a very good singer and musician and we have often done concerts together. He is an Israeli citizen.

The original sin is occupation

The political situation is really bad. Sometimes I get to a point where I cannot see, literally speaking, a glimpse of hope of anything around here. I am disappointed in the Palestinian Authority. I think they were not able to lead the nation towards a better future. Our leadership disappointed all of us, both the Palestinian people who live directly under occupation, and the Arab Palestinians living within the state of Israel. So I am worried about the future. If we talk about the future state of Palestine I have lots of questions as to what it will be like. How will it be ruled? Who is going to lead?

The original sin is occupation; Israel and its policy towards the Palestinians and their policy within the West Bank has not changed. When it comes to the daily lives of the people, nothing has changed. I believe that Israel does not believe in a peaceful and just solution for the Palestinian people. I think that peace with the Palestinians is not a strategic plan or vision for the state of Israel. The past two to three years have been completely different from what we believed or spoke about five, six, seven years ago. Things have changed tremendously in terms of the political situation. More and more people have emigrated.

Treated like animals

I worry about the Christian minority living within the West Bank; many Christian families are leaving because people feel that there is no hope. People are being treated so badly at checkpoints by Israeli soldiers. I was in Ramallah last week attending an ordination of one of our deacons in Ramallah. Getting out of Ramallah was like hell – we were treated like animals. I thought of those Palestinians who have to cross this checkpoint every day and it shocked me. Immediately, those people came to my mind, standing in long queues waiting for their turn to come to the checkpoint and speak with the soldier who is 17 or 18 years old, giving orders of what to do and what not to do. I feel it is hopeless.

The churches' role: to build bridges of peace

I think as a Church we should not give up our role in terms of working, preaching and speaking about peace and the way we understand peace. The situation is one side of the story, but the other side of the story is that the Church has to continue in its role of trying to build bridges of peace. The times we are going to fail are much, much more than the times we are going to succeed, but that is what the gospel is all about. The situation should not make us give up our beliefs and our stands and our theology. We need to speak honestly with no fear because if we lose this prophetic voice then the Church has lost everything. We have to be a prophetic voice despite the hopeless situation.

What the prophetic voice says

I think the prophetic voice is saying to the people of Palestine and Gaza and West Bank, we should not give up our cause and our right to have a better future in the land where we were born; the land where our ancestors lived and cultivated their land and took care of their olive trees.

I think the Church also has to bring practical solutions and practical support to those people – financial support and housing projects. We cannot speak up only on theories and preach about theories; we have to go down and help people to stay – build more institutions and have more job opportunities for people in order to buy their daily bread and live in dignity. We have to find them places they can live. I think our Church is doing a tremendous job in terms of helping people to build a true sense of belonging. I am proud of what the Church is doing in the West Bank, in Gaza, in Nablus, in Ramallah where we have Anglican churches or institutions. We are small, but day after day I am sure God will open our eyes towards new ways through which we help the people whether Christians or Muslims to build up a stronger sense of belonging to the land, to the place, to the culture and the history.

Bethlehem Speaks

The problems of Arab/Palestinian Israelis

Our people who live within the state of Israel have many issues we have to deal with in terms of our relationship with the state of Israel and their policy towards our people. As a priest I have to answer lots of questions from my people within the state of Israel because they have lots of worries and fears about their future.

There are so many things in common between us and our brothers and sisters in the West Bank, but in a different package, because we carry an Israeli passport and live within the state of Israel, but young people are afraid of their future. They do not know what is going to happen. Many of our young people have lost hope about a better future, because they know if they go to university they will graduate, come out into the world, and have no place. It is the worst feeling ever when you feel that you have no place in the society where you live, where you have been brought up, where you were born.

So I have to have a message to bring hope to those people here within the state of Israel – find them places to live, work on housing projects, find them job opportunities, because unemployment is getting bigger and bigger even within the Arab sector here in the state of Israel. In my parish I have families where I have to take care of their monthly income. I have to find them financial resources in order to help them send their kids to schools and just buy them food every month. People have no jobs, because they are not first priority when it comes to jobs. We are the last priority.

I think Israel economically speaking is struggling. I know lots of Jewish friends who are really desperate, and I meet with Jewish friends who work with my wife Hanna who think the same way we think as Arabs; they want to leave the state. Some of those Jewish friends are new immigrants; they were promised a better life in the state of Israel but it turned out to be different. Diplomacy, economics, the political situation has been a big disappointment to people, even Jewish people, not only Arab Palestinian people.

My call to the churches: wake up!

It is time for you to wake up. I do not know how long the western Church and people will continue in their sleep in terms of their awareness and their understanding of what is really happening on the ground in this part of the world.

The West, and the Church in the West, has gone into a very, very, very long sleep. It is time to wake up and support the people, especially their brothers and sisters, the Christians; I am not afraid of saying support the Palestinian Christians; I am not denying the right of Muslims to live, but Muslims – and this is a credit to them – are much stronger than us Arab Christians when it comes to belonging to the land. It is the easiest thing for a Christian family to buy a ticket, take an aeroplane and leave. I think we need to learn from Muslims and their strong sense of belonging to the land, their strong sense of belonging to their history, and their olive trees, and the soil of their land.

But Christians in this part of the world are a minority and feel that they are forgotten. We are sometimes accused by our Muslim brothers and sisters of supporting the policies of the West – the policies of the United States and Britain and their policies in the Middle East. They see us as western and as representing Bush and

Blair's policies. Yet for the West, we do not exist. So we are lost and I want people to come to understand, especially in the West. If you think of us as just guardians of holy shrines and bellringers on Sundays and that is it, you are mistaken. We are not guardians of the shrines. We are not here to preserve those nice places for you to come and visit, so you can feel the place and cry because of those feelings.

We are a community which has been here for hundreds of years, two thousand years, working and witnessing to the cause of Christ. We want people to come and meet with our people, worship with them on Sunday. Meet with them for a fellowship after a Sunday service in the parish halls. Eat, talk, dance, party with them. That is how people could really support our people. And I am not talking about financial support. That is part of it but when we talk of support, there are so many ways to support the people and the Church to continue to do the work which has been done for two thousand years. So wake up; you Christians in the West have to come to understand that it is your responsibility. It is there on your shoulders, and you cannot say, 'We have nothing to do with this.' It is your role, it is your mission, and it is your call to support your brothers and sisters in this part of the world where it all began.

Witness 7: Nael Abu Rahman
The heart tells us how to treat others

Nael is priest in charge of St Andrew's, Ramallah, Palestine, but still helps at St George's Cathedral, East Jerusalem, as well. Nael was 28 when I interviewed him in May 2007. He is the youngest Anglican priest in the Diocese of Jerusalem.

The worldwide Church and also the local churches meet and talk about the situation but they do not do enough. We, as clergy and bishops, have to do something more. I just had a copy of a report from Sabeel (the ecumenical liberation theology group based in Jerusalem) about the situation, about the number of Christians in every city and every village and how much difficulty they have and how many people have left the country. All bishops and all heads of churches have received a copy of this, but what did they do after seeing it? I hope they read it first, because if you read it you cannot just put it with the other books and not do something.

Behind the wall in Ramallah

It is good to compare Ramallah and Bethlehem. There is more life in Ramallah. I think there is more life than in East Jerusalem. There are coffee shops and people at restaurants, Wonderful! I like that! After the youth group meeting we go to have something in one of the coffee shops there and it is wonderful. So there are many restaurants and you see people walking, but even with all these things they still tell you how many years they have not come to Jerusalem, and it is only 20 kilometres away. It is really sad how they need this permit to go out from Ramallah, and it is very sad when walking around Ramallah to see the wall.

It is very sad also to see the Israeli army in Ramallah catching somebody and taking them, and nobody says anything. They come in; they take somebody or kill them and go out. You can see people going out with each other and walking or going to church, going to different parties, but inside them there is sadness.

They used to go to Jerusalem but they cannot now. For Christians and for Muslims, it is important to come to Jerusalem and to worship in Jerusalem. People from all over the world come here to visit this land of the Holy One, yet people just a few kilometres away, even from Bethlehem, cannot come.

The Church is leaving

One of the essential needs here is housing. People do not have anywhere to live so they move. People do not have a job or receive a good salary, and how then do they support children and educate them? So it is all connected: job, house and money – all together. We cannot tell people to stay in this land saying 'this is your land, this is the land of our Lord Jesus Christ', without offering them something.

Through the people you find Christ

This is our land – we were born here. It is important for Christians because if we say that Jesus Christ, the Son of God, came down from heaven and lived in this land, and now we as his disciples and his followers leave this land, then when people come from Britain, or from all over the world, they will only visit churches as buildings and stones and maybe as museums. Maybe you will find monks in some of the churches because they keep the churches open and cleaned, but you will not find people to meet. The expression 'the living stones' became very popular, and we need to see the holiness through the people living here.

I hope every pilgrim will come here and seek and find the face of Christ through the local people. You are our sisters and brothers in Christ because we share the same faith, the same God, the same Lord, the same sacraments, the same Bible.

So you should come here and meet me as well.

You should come here and meet my parishioners.

You should come here and meet our schools and the students in our schools, in different institutions and in youth groups.

But visit the people, because through the people you find Christ.

Let us start talking about the same Lord, the same Jesus, who was born in Bethlehem, the specific town of Bethlehem. The people living here, especially the Christians, are important because they live, keep the holy places and worship in the birthplace of my Lord and your Lord. So the faith link is the first point that has to be important.

But we cannot forget how they live inside Bethlehem and how it is difficult from outside Bethlehem for local people even to visit this place. It may be easier for you to come from outside this country to go and visit Bethlehem, easier for you than people from Jerusalem or from Ramallah or from Nablus or different parts of this country, even from inside Israel – for Christians from inside Israel it is difficult.

So we have to think about how it was difficult for Jesus even to be born in Bethlehem, because we know from the Gospels that those who were originally from Bethlehem had to be there to register and everything was full. It was not easy to find a place for Jesus to be born. So also today, it is still difficult to go and find where Jesus was born.

Have we got hearts of stone?

It is important to tell Olmert (the Israeli Prime Minister) or any leader in the world, 'Just be a human being'. Let us forget for a minute you are the prime minister and let us talk about a soldier or somebody in the army who is driving a tank; I just saw a picture of a tank driver who did not stop and drove through children throwing stones and killed them. I can never understand how they cannot feel anything and how they forget this is a human being. They killed the children, and they did that many times. They did that in Gaza to a foreigner even. So where are their hearts? I think sometimes we have arrived at a point where we have hearts of stone. The Bible in Ezekiel says, 'I will take from you your heart of stone and give you a heart of flesh', a heart that can think and love and can treat people as human beings.

You cannot be a human being if you do not follow your heart of love.

So this is what I would say to Ehud Olmert and to others, to anyone who is a leader – use your heart. As a human being, I will love others and will be just and think about the rights of others. I would tell him to work for justice, for reconciliation and peace. These three words are important for any leader: peace, justice and reconciliation. We cannot work for those things if we have a heart of stone, or if we have no heart. So the heart is very important; it tells us how to treat others, how to think, how to love, how to respect others, and how to give others their rights while keeping our own rights as well.

5

God is not a racist God

———•◆•———

Palestinians are humans too
They weep and they bleed like me and like you
We can treat them like outcasts as so many do
But Palestinians are humans too.

If an Israeli dies, we mourn as we should
If they're American or British, we know that they're good
But when it comes to Arabs and Muslims too
We turn a little racist – but I've got some news.

Palestinians are humans too.

Garth Hewitt

Witness 8: Jonathan Kuttab

This chapter is given over to one voice – Jonathan Kuttab. Jonathan is a Christian lawyer and a human rights activist. He studied in the USA and is a member of the Bar there. He came back, studied Hebrew and joined the Israeli Bar Association as well as the Palestinian one. He has been very active in human rights as well as his private law practice. He says, 'I am a deeply committed Christian and that is what motivates all of my behaviour and action. I take my faith very seriously'.

Very close to complete segregation

I believe that we are very close to the finalization of long-term Israeli projects, aimed at institutionalizing the occupation as a permanent state of affairs with complete segregation between Jews and Arabs within the occupied territories.

It is a form of apartheid, but in some sense it is much worse. The wall is perhaps the latest manifestation, but there are other elements that were there all along and that everybody has observed and declared to be illegal all along, for example, the exclusively Jewish settlements. These are not Israeli residences because Israeli Arabs are not allowed to stay there. They are exclusively Jewish settlements. Also the various attempts at designating a local Palestinian authority – deferring to it responsibility for running the affairs of the Arabs – but without giving it genuine power and sovereignty is a problem. The establishment of two parallel systems of schools, of health care, of social benefits, of laws, of courts, and most recently of roads – one for the Jewish population and one for the Arab population; these are other examples. This is an ongoing process that started right after 1967. But right now I think we are approaching the finalization and the fruition of this scheme; together with a particular push to get Palestinian approval or acquiescence through some form of peace agreement that will be heralded to the whole world as a final solution of the whole problem, the way the withdrawal from Gaza was heralded as the end of the occupation there, when in fact it was not.

The dangerous myth that this part of the world is unique

I think that it operates on a number of levels. The first level, and perhaps the most dangerous, is the idea that somehow Israel or this part of the world is unique and that normal expectations, normal rules, normal standards of human behaviour do not apply here. This is unique so we have to set up our own unique system. That was a central element of the Oslo Agreements. It emphatically and specifically said international law does not apply here. So this is a new arrangement that the parties will agree to by themselves. Somehow Israel, because the Jews are special, because of the Holocaust, because of their security situation, because of biblical or divine mandate – for whatever reason – is special and unique, and what applies to the rest of the world does not apply here.

The rejection and abhorrence of militarism, for example, which Christians should agree to throughout the world, here it is different. The opposition to nuclear weapons and other weapons of mass destruction, which Christians champion throughout the world – even in their own countries – simply does not apply to the state of Israel. It is different.

The rejection of discrimination and theocracies and religious-based political systems does not happen here. We object to it in Iran. We object to it in Afghanistan. People resent it in their own country when it looks like there is too much influence of religion over politics. But Israel somehow is allowed to openly declare itself to be a Jewish state that can systematically and legally discriminate against non-Jews and its own citizens.

Israel is not subject to the same rules as everyone else

Somehow Israel is different. They are not subject to the same rules that apply to everyone else. So this is one thing that we have to bear in mind even when making comparisons with apartheid. In my view, this situation is quite different and far worse than apartheid. But the central objection to the comparison with apartheid is that there is a sense of legitimacy to a Jewish state that does not exist to a Muslim state or to a white state in South Africa, or to an otherwise racist state anywhere in the world. The Jews are entitled somehow, because of the suffering, religion, or because of the uniqueness of their history and anti-Semitism. The rules and the laws that apply to the rest of humanity do not necessarily apply to them in the same way.

However, I think the central message is that you are not doing Jews or anybody else a favour by accepting this paradigm of uniqueness. God loves all of his children. In fact one of the central things that Jesus did was a sort of systematic de-Zionization of the Old Testament. He completely erased and undermined the idea that Jews are special, that you are Abraham's children and that therefore you have special privileges. As a Jew, Jesus said, 'Stop all of that – God does not favour a particular tribe over others. You are not uniquely better than anybody else. You do not have any entitlements. There is nothing particularly sacred about this land. God is spirit and those who worship him must worship him in spirit and in truth, not necessarily in Jerusalem or Samaria or anywhere else.'

So Jesus was systematically opening up God's plan of salvation – the gospel – to the whole world. Now I think that that is a good thing. Not just for everybody else, for us Gentiles, but it is good also for Jews to be treated as God's children – no worse, but no better than anyone else.

The sin of anti-Semitism

The sin of anti-Semitism is that it treated Jews as worse, as if they were different, somehow less human than the rest of the human race. I suspect that much of what is happening in Israel now is the other side of the same sin – somehow treating Jews as a super-race, as a people apart, as distinct, not quite subject to the same rules as everyone else. I do not think that that does the Jews a favour. I think that Jews do have their religion, their traditions and their identity; nobody should deny them that. But when you combine that with political demands and requirements of exclusivity rather than generality, I think you fall into trouble.

A call to religious leaders

The first thing that I would ask of religious leaders is that they be true to their own values of their own faith and not try to moderate or change their positions to suit their audience or suit what they would like.

If I object to terrorism or if I object to torture or if I think that racism is bad, I ought to stick by that belief regardless of who the perpetrator is and who the victim is. I do not take that position because I sympathize with a particular set of victims and if somebody else is being victimized I let it continue. And I do not take those positions only when my enemies are the evildoers, but also when my friends and supporters and my own country carry out these practices; I do not downplay it and try to excuse it. So my first requirement for religious leaders is that they be consistent with their own moral values and be willing to apply them without fear or favour no matter what the situation is. When you do that, tremendous results follow. You will find that you need to be a little sharp with some of your friends sometimes, rather than accommodating. You will find yourself saying the same things that somebody that you may not like is saying because it happens to be true. If the most evil person in the world proclaims that the earth is round, it does not mean that I have to deny that the earth is round simply because this person believes so.

I must be willing to maintain it because I believe it to be true though some very unpleasant people may be saying the same thing. I think this is what happened recently with Jimmy Carter when he talked about apartheid and Israel. People said, 'Oh, you are just like all of these anti-Semites, you are like David Duke from the Ku Klux Klan who also says this is apartheid.' But the issue is not who says it – the issue is whether it fits the criteria or not, whether in fact it does discriminate, whether in fact it does oppress, if it is morally abhorrent or not. I cringe when I think that I will be forced into the same position as some people that I do not like. But I must take that position because I believe in it and I must not steer away from it because some unsavoury characters happen to believe the same thing.

There is a blessing when you are falsely accused

I would like religious leaders to stand up for peace, not for violence. I would like them to stand up for non-discrimination, for openness rather than exclusivity. I would like them to speak up for equality rather than for the privilege of a particular group. I would like them to promote genuine co-operation rather than subjugation and submission to an oppressive situation. I would like them to speak for justice – to be a voice of prophecy.

Now, in this particular situation given the history of the area, I am afraid that it takes much more courage to speak out against the Israelis or in favour of the Palestinians. Not that I am saying that they need to be partisan. But what

I am saying is that they should be consistent with their moral views even if it puts them in opposition to some very powerful forces. Even if it makes them sympathize and appear to be in the same camp as those who are weak and helpless, as the Palestinians are these days. In other words, you know there is a special blessing in the Beatitudes: 'Blessed are you if they say all manner of evil things against you falsely for my name.' Most people are afraid to address this issue because they are afraid of being accused of anti-Semitism. But if they speak up and if they are not really anti-Semitic then there is a huge blessing there for them because they will be reviled and they will be accused falsely of anti-Semitism. Now if they are really anti-Semitic and cannot stand Jews then there is no blessing in it for them and they need to repent from that sin. But if they are genuinely open and genuinely willing to see the evil that is being perpetrated, and they are willing to speak in favour of justice for the Palestinians, then when they are being called anti-Semitic falsely, there is a great blessing awaiting them.

The system of hafrada – *separate but not equal*

Things are getting worse rather than better. There is no question that what we see is a systematic process of subjugating the Palestinians, setting in place a system of *hafrada,* the Hebrew word for segregation or separation.

'Apartheid' was not necessarily a curse word until the world realized what it was doing. Apartheid was allowing people to live apart in different areas and be with their own people, suggesting that that is the way they like it. So *hafrada* also says let the Arabs live 'separately' from the Jews. So the wall is intended to create *hafrada.* The Jewish settlements are an expression of *hafrada.* Separate roads are *hafrada*. Again, this system of *hafrada*, of segregation or separation is becoming institutionalized and there is nothing equal about it. It is not separate but equal; it is separate and totally unequal.

The Palestinian community is being fragmented and segmented. The West Bank alone has 93 separate enclaves and you cannot move between one and the other without going through some kind of Israeli obstacle, a checkpoint, either with soldiers who will allow or not allow you to go through, or physical barriers that you have to climb over and carry your goods and your sick and your young over because otherwise you cannot get through. There are 93 different enclaves and about 276 separate checkpoints or barriers throughout the area. And we are not talking here about what separates the West Bank from Israel.

Unfair to call this apartheid – it is much worse

So there is no question about any security basis for it. This is separating Palestinian areas from one another so that there cannot be any real economic life, social life, cultural life, health services, proper education, interaction or family life, when you physically cannot move around between the areas. I am not even talking about cutting them off from East Jerusalem or from Israel itself or from the outside world – just within the confines of the West Bank, and it is a tiny area. People who look at maps need to look at the scale on the maps and they will be horrified how small the areas are within which the Palestinians have to exist. The smallest, tiniest joke of a Bantustan in South Africa was bigger than the entire West Bank. My South African friends tell me it is totally unfair to compare this to apartheid. It is unfair to South Africa because this is so much worse. You cannot compare it.

68

Right now we have a structure, a very weird structure that puts the health, education and welfare of the population under the control of the Palestinian Authority yet does not allow the Palestinian Authority even to have its own taxes and customs; these are collected for it by the Israelis. They cannot even get the aid from donor countries without Israeli permission. Now I am not a fan of Hamas, but they were elected in the last elections. I hope they will be defeated in the next elections, but in the meantime all government services, all government employees, the entire population, is being criminalized, demonized and strangled because of what happened in the elections; yet this process, the Israeli strangulation and refusal to turn over the taxes, started even before the elections took place.

So the population is left in limbo. We cannot have our own leadership, yet we are not under direct Israeli occupation and control. We are told that we run ourselves or our own affairs, yet we are not allowed to run our own affairs any way we like, and the daily suffering is tremendous. It is an accumulation of obstacles, humiliations, restrictions, frustrations that I am pretty sure are unmatched anywhere in the world. There are other places in the world where there is more poverty, other places where there may be more brutality of one particular kind or another. But the accumulation of oppression at every level that is widespread throughout the whole population, I do not know any place in the world where we have this situation.

There are very supportive Israelis

There are Israelis who are very supportive, who are very worried about what is happening, who are morally

69

outraged, some of them to the point of leaving the country because they cannot stand it any more, but they are not really in leadership positions. There are a number of reporters like Amira Hass and Gideon Levy and others who very bravely report on the reality so that if an Israeli really wants to know, he or she can read the reports in *Ha'aretz* and elsewhere (that you will never see in English, by the way). They describe the situation in great depth and detail and accuracy. Incidentally, the Israeli press is much, much more open than the international press or the world press or the Jewish press in the world.

We need to condemn attacks on civilians

We Palestinians have our own faults. We need to be much more articulate about what we want and how we want to achieve it. We need to be clearer and more consistent in condemning attacks on civilians. There is a lot of non-violent action taking place, non-violent resistance to the wall – for instance, Sami Awad in the Bethlehem region [who runs training workshops in non-violence through the Holy Land Trust] and the Bi'lin [a village being cut off from its land by the wall] people and others.

Unfortunately, though, we are captured by the rhetoric of violence, of the gun; we glorify the gun. Even Hamas, for a whole year and a half, before the elections, refrained from carrying out any military activity. Yet they kept up a continuing stream of vitriolic, blood-curdling propaganda and so they did not achieve any of the benefits of having refrained from armed struggle for a year and a half; it was only Fatah who was carrying out military activities at that time.

So I do not want to exonerate us as Palestinians. We are to blame for a lot of what is happening. However, the oppressive conditions under which we are living, in Gaza for example, are devastating – Gaza is just one huge pressure cooker. You get 1.5 million people on a very tiny piece of land, barely 30 kilometres by 10.

You deny them access to the sea. You deny them access to the outside world. They cannot have agriculture because you have cut off the water. You are not allowing industry to thrive, or imports and exports. You are cutting them off even from the West Bank, totally and completely. Now the only thing that gets in are weapons. What do you expect?

You put three or four cats in a small room and lock them in and see what happens after twenty-four hours; they turn vicious and start attacking each other and everyone else who dares to set foot in the room.

Having said that, I would say that Palestinians still need to articulate more clearly a non-violent, moral, legally based opposition to the occupation than they have been doing so far.

I would say that at the political level there has been a lot of maturity and growth in the Palestinian community. The majority of Palestinians today are open to a realistic, pragmatic compromise that gives them less than 20 per cent of the area of Palestine. But we are not getting any kind of response from the other side. This would look like the West Bank and Gaza, hopefully with a corridor between them.

I would say the settlements would need to be back in Palestine as well, and I would say that that is a very moderate view. Right now this view is accepted by the vast majority of Palestinians. The majority of Palestinians also do not think there is any point to the Qassam rocket attacks.

In May 2007 something happened that nobody even noticed. Hamas issued its new declaration – its new constitution and it had taken out all reference to the destruction of the state of Israel. This was a historic occasion. They were talking about getting ready for the new elections and becoming more acceptable to the international community. Now, they do not broadcast it because they are still caught up in the rhetoric of armed struggle and of liberating all of Palestine. But there are some very significant changes taking place even within Hamas.

On the Christian community

The Christian community is as St Paul said, beaten, but not down and out – beaten but not destroyed. I think the Palestinian community continues to be steadfast. The numbers are decreasing. The hope for the future is decreasing. Many families who are willing to suffer themselves are not willing to have their children face a future of continual suffering and lack of a horizon. So many of them are emigrating. But those who are still here are doing wonderful work just by their physical presence, by their involvement with different institutions and ministries and services. Those who are in education and health and human rights and in community life are doing work far out of proportion to their numbers. Palestinian Muslims feel this – I was just reading an article by a Muslim about how terrible and dangerous it is for the Palestinian community that so many Palestinian Christians are leaving. In many ways we are the salt of the earth when it comes to Palestine. We do not see ourselves as a minority here. We see ourselves as an integral part of the Palestinian community but we do contribute in special and unique ways.

I would like to think that those who are Christians here, even those who are only nominally Christian, have a certain quality that they have absorbed through their religious training, through their schools, from their parents. Even though they may not be active churchgoers themselves, they do reflect a certain quality of public spirit, of honesty, of integrity, of service. I think the Muslims realize that that is true. They realize that it would be a great loss to all of us if the Christian community keeps shrinking the way it has been shrinking. A number of things are needed to stop the community shrinking: some are economic – in terms of economic opportunities – some educational, some to do with housing.

Move from theology of racism to theology of love

But a lot of it has to do with a sense of solidarity. We need to feel the Christian world is with us and feels our pain and agony, rather than that the Christian world is blindly supportive of Israel and does so claiming that they are doing it as Christians. They claim that somehow the Bible dictates that they stand with the oppressor over the oppressed, with the occupier over the occupied, and that really hurts when we need to explain and defend ourselves to our fellow Christians abroad. Also we have to explain to our fellow Muslims that these positions that they hear are not the true voice of Christianity, that Christian Zionism does not in fact reflect what the Bible teaches; that God is not a racist God. He did not give this land to the Jews. He does not support the eviction and, basically, ethnic cleansing of Palestinians.

The heart of the problem is that throughout the Old Testament without any doubt it does describe a campaign of ethnic cleansing. Joshua would go and kill every man, woman and child totally and completely. In Hebrew it is called the commandment of genocide. If somebody reads the Old Testament selectively and applies what that says to the modern-day state of Israel then obviously they will arrive at the conclusion of justifying exclusivity, racism, colonialism, oppression and ethnic cleansing. I would like to think, though, that we can read the Old Testament through the eyes of Jesus or through the eyes of God as he declared himself through Jesus.

That particular hermeneutic allows us to move away from a theology of genocide and exclusivity and racism towards a theology of universalism, openness, love, reconciliation, the kingdom of God, a new reality, reconciling God and humanity, and human with fellow human. Reconciliation through Christ leads us into a new reality where it is not about heavenly kingdoms and areas of real estate and theocracies that are the goals of Christians. But rather it is about the kingdom of God in our hearts, in our actions, in our behaviour, in our attitudes towards others, including those who are not of the same faith.

I think it is a whole different hermeneutic through which you need to read the Old Testament. You cannot throw out the Old Testament. You must keep it, but you must read it with new eyes. On the other hand you cannot take portions of it that are repudiated by Jews today and take them as normative for your behaviour. I was surprised when I was at a Seder where they talked about the ten plagues of Egypt and I told them this is very interesting. You go through a very convoluted process of reinterpretation to soften the wrath of God against Egyptians – to say that you wish that they did not have to suffer that much. You spill a few drops of wine because your joy at liberation has to be tempered with the grief of the Egyptians whose firstborn children will die. I said this theology, this attempt to interpret the Old Testament to make it more palatable and more acceptable to our modern world, is different from Christians today who are reaching back into the Old Testament to justify warmongering; to justify their oppression by quoting the 'Lord of hosts' and the 'God of armies' and what Joshua did, and calling for victory in battle. So this is a strange flip-flop. I think we need to know how to read the Old Testament. We need to read it through New Testament eyes.

The way of prayer

One of the most important things people can do is pray. I do not mean by prayer what you do in your closet between you and God and then you forget about it. I think about prayer as an attempt to align ourselves with God's will in a particular situation. So if people start praying truly for the peace of Jerusalem, start praying for their leaders, start praying for their churches, start praying for their brothers and sisters in the Holy Land, start praying for Palestinians and for Jews – for both of them – I think that there will be consequences to that.

There will be consequences in terms of positions they take, in terms of how they read their newspaper and what they write to their editors or in their newspapers; in how they relate to other people within their community on these issues. Eventually I think, just like in South Africa, the situation will change when there is an international groundswell of rejection of the evil here, and solidarity with those who are struggling for peace and justice.

Recently, British academics took a step of boycott. Others take steps of disinvestment; the Anglican Church has considered disinvesting from companies that are directly related to the oppression, to the building of walls or to the settlements. Sanctions I think are going to be important. Also we need a different type of tourism in the Holy Land. A tourism that is open not only to seeing the holy places, but also to meeting the people of the land; a tourism that is willing to come and stay in Bethlehem and not listen to the tourist guides that tell them, 'It is too dangerous, do not go there'. We need tourists who are willing to come and visit the people here, in solidarity, in fellowship: to worship with them, to talk to them, to see them and, ultimately, to support them.

It also requires building bridges in your own country: in Britain, for example, not only with the Arab and Muslim community there, but also with the Jewish community; but to do so in a very responsible fashion. Unfortunately most Christian–Jewish dialogue has concentrated on avoiding issues of justice, avoiding issues of Palestine/Israel. They concentrate on tolerance, being against missionaries, understanding the Old Testament and the special relationship to the land, in talking about the Holocaust and the burden of guilt. All of that is important, but now we have also to talk about justice. We have to talk about occupation. We have to talk about the oppression of Palestinians. We have to talk about the moral imperatives of the Old and the New Testaments when it comes to peace in the Holy Land, and to violence and what that means.

So I think there is a lot in Britain that needs to be done, both with the Jewish and with the Arab and Muslim communities there.

Anti-Arab and Muslim racism

Right now also, throughout the world, we see a great rise of a new kind of anti-Semitism against Muslims – it is anti-Arab, anti-Muslim Islamophobia, which manifests itself in very ugly ways; sometimes subtle, but sometimes very blatant ways in the press, in cartoons, in the job market. In the daily social lives of Muslims and Arabs in Europe and in the United States there is a lot of anti-Arab and anti-Muslim racism. This is no less evil than anti-Semitism against Jews, and I think it should be fought.

6

Don't let Bethlehem die

One of us – flesh and blood
Reaching out a touch of love
Breaking walls that divide
God with us bringing alive

In a manger in a cave
A humble birth and lives are changed
By the news God comes to earth
With the poor and shows their worth

Had no place to lay his head
Never had a rich man's bed
He was despised and outcast too
Wounds and pain was what he knew

One of us – flesh and blood
Reaching out a touch of love
Breaking walls that divide
God with us bringing alive
                            Garth Hewitt

In this chapter, more witnesses speak.

Witness 9: Jad Isaac
Bethlehem is dying

Jad Isaac is the Director General of the Applied Research Institute, Jerusalem (ARIJ) in the West Bank. He directs the Palestinian Institute, researching on agriculture, environment and water. We had this conversation in front of a map of the Bethlehem area and you can tell he is pointing to it.

Like separating twins

Let me give you these striking figures: 87 per cent of the Bethlehem government area is under Israeli control; about 94 per cent of the population are confined to 13 per cent of Bethlehem. This means that Bethlehem has become a ghetto. Israelis come and raid Bethlehem during the night, every night, often arresting somebody. During the last five years, what has happened to Bethlehem is that Israel started its process with the wall of segregating Bethlehem from Jerusalem. This is the first time in history that Bethlehem and Jerusalem have been segregated from each other. It is like separating twins. The minute this wall started coming up, you saw its impact on every aspect of life and Bethlehem is dying. There is no life in it because of the wall and its ghettoization. Remember that in the partition plan of 1947 Jerusalem and Bethlehem were all part of the *corpus separatum* which is supposed to be under international trustees. The *corpus separatum* included all of Bethlehem's land and of course both East and West Jerusalem.

I will give you some examples of the effect of the wall. Many of the doctors in Bethlehem used to work in hospitals in Jerusalem, but no longer do. Most of the teachers in Jerusalem came from the Bethlehem area.

79

Now because of the difficulty in getting permits to get to Jerusalem, all the schools in Jerusalem are facing a severe crisis; there are no staff to fill the vacancies. At the same time there were several Jerusalemites who were teaching at Bethlehem University who now have a difficult time every time they come; the wait for so many hours at checkpoints is making life unbearable. Also the Israeli plan for the next two years is to build a wall of settlements which goes parallel to the existing wall, totally severing any relationship between Bethlehem and Jerusalem. I do not know why the western Church is silent about this.

Deals between the Church and the Israeli Defence Force (IDF)

In many cases the path of the wall was changed because of deals between church leaders and the IDF, so that the land confiscated behind the wall does not include any Christian land. For instance Cremisan [a monastery and winery] was never part of Jerusalem. Cremisan has always been, historically, part of Beit Jala. Cremisan now will be isolated. It will be inaccessible to the people of Beit Jala. This is something we cannot understand.

I think it shows how narrow-minded are those in the church establishment. They preach on Sundays about love or about justice and they talk about peace. But there cannot be peace in the Holy Land without justice. And justice cannot be achieved through walls, confiscation and land grabs. The wall goes around Cremisan, so look at Beit Jala; it is becoming a ghetto with no open space left. This was the only green space left for the Christians of Beit Jala; it has been taken out by the wall. If the wall had gone around it, it would have been included, then all this land would have been available to the people of Beit Jala.

The churches are silent

If you look at Bethlehem now there is no open space left for anyone. It is becoming like a refugee camp. It is the strangulation of Bethlehem. What will happen when the population grows? The Christian residents of Bethlehem, Beit Sahour and Beit Jala will sell their lands and leave. The churches are silent about it. We have the lowest percentage of Christians among all the Middle Eastern countries. In the Holy Land we have the lowest percentage of Christians, compared with Egypt, Jordan, Syria, Lebanon, Iraq. Why don't the churches think about this? How did it happen? The decline has been associated with the establishment of the state of Israel and the occupation after the 1967 war ended.

The Israelis would love to have everybody here labelled as Muslim terrorists so these Palestinian Christians are not needed. Remember, any attempts to put us in a sanctuary means we will become extinct. So we do not need special favouritism. We want to be left alone and the violations against us by Israel to be stopped. We have been here for ages and they do not understand us. I do not want to move anywhere else. I do not want to be anywhere else in the world except here in Bethlehem where my family has been here for four hundred years or more.

They are taking the heart

The impact of the settlements is affecting the infrastructure of Bethlehem. There was never a direct transportation line that linked Bethlehem with Ramallah, never in history. To go to Ramallah, you go to Jerusalem first. From

Bethlehem, Beit Sahour or Beit Jala, you go to Jerusalem. In Jerusalem you take public transport to Ramallah or Nablus or anywhere. Now this has stopped. Even going to Jericho, we used to go from Bethlehem via Jerusalem. Now in the absence of this, the only way left to us is to go through the Wadi – the Kidron Valley road (the 'road of fire') which takes ages, with lots of checkpoints and lots of hardship.

Israel did not come up with any turnpike or transit way because they want the Palestinians to forget Jerusalem. That is why they are building the wall in such a way. They are taking the heart. Through this wall, they are taking Jerusalem out of the game. So now every time a Bethlehemite wants to get to Ramallah, they will have to go all the way around on the 'road of fire' to get to Ramallah.

Historically we were never part of Hebron, and we do not want to be part of Hebron because we will be absorbed. In Hebron there are 600,000 people. In all of Bethlehem there are 170,000 and, historically, education- ally, socially we are associated with Jerusalem. I con- sidered myself to be a Jerusalem man. If I want to buy a new shirt, a good one, I go to Jerusalem. If I want to have a decent meal, I go to Jerusalem. That is what we used to do. But for the past six years I could not go to Jerusalem with my family; this was not part of any nightmare we could have imagined.

We will not accept it

There is no open space left. Pollution is very high. There is no place for any dumping site. Now the World Bank is saying let us strike a deal and find a dump that will serve Bethlehem and Hebron. This summer was a very hot summer but water only comes every two weeks, and it is our water, but Israel controls it.

Immediately following 1967 they issued a military order that all water viaducts in the area of Judaea and Samaria are to be under the control of the office in charge of the civil administration.

The Oslo Agreement said that Israel recognizes the Palestinian water rights, and that these rights will be discussed and agreed upon in final negotiations. But so far, no negotiations have taken place on water rights. Every time we bring the issue up, they delay it. They have taken it by force, this is not their right, we will not accept it, and we will not accept either the Bush declaration that Israel has to retain six settlement blocs in the West Bank. This is not the business of justice. We will not accept the Jordan Valley to be inaccessible to us; we will not accept the corridors which they are contemplating. It has to be either a fully contiguous, viable Palestinian state or why strike a deal?

The settlers

Why should Israel be allowed to get away with violations of international law which says that settlements are illegal? The settlements are a contradiction of international law and they should be removed. There are 500,000 settlers – 10 per cent of Jews in Israel are settlers, including six Knesset members and two ministers. And a lot of the army generals are helping them. But at the same time, Israel was able to accommodate 300,000 Russian immigrants during the 1990s. So they can accommodate the 500,000 settlers in one year inside Israel. No problem. It is not their land, and justice says that they have to leave.

We want to be like every other nation

Tony Blair is negotiating, focusing on trying to bring industrial zones, as if he does not learn from history. He wants to build here some joint industrial zones to bring Israeli industries and help Palestinian workers find jobs, pouring in money so this will calm people. Yes, there is a lot of poverty but once we get food we want recognition, we want statehood, we want to be like every other nation in the world. We want to feel that we belong to the family of the nations. I want to have a Palestinian airline to be able to travel to anywhere. I do not want to have the Israelis check me every time I go out. I do not want to see their faces on the checkpoints. I go to Ramallah three or four times a week; I spend now half of what is left of my life on checkpoints. I do not want this life. I could be doing something more useful.

What justice would look like

So the first issue is justice – justice for the Palestinians, and an end to the occupation. We want free space. We want to enjoy life. I want to drive my car with my kids and my grandkids, to be able to travel around. I want to see water. I want to see agricultural production. I want to see schools. I want to see playgrounds, villages, theatres, opera houses and a museum. Where is the Palestinian natural history museum or zoo? I want to see these. An opera house! I would love to see a Palestinian opera house established somewhere. But there is no open space left for us.

A recipe for disaster

Since the year 2000 and the beginning of the intifada, 1.4 million trees have been cut down. Sharon ordered most of the cutting of trees. You should see what happened in Gaza. A large area has been denuded totally. And now 24 per cent of the Gaza strip is a free fire zone. Anything that moves is shot down immediately and killed; the children, a donkey, a car – anything that moves within this area. They are firing from above with drones which take zero-time shots at everything they find moving – boom! You are dead. You shoot and ask questions later.

The Israelis should get a training course on the environment to know the meaning of 'sustainability'. What is the meaning of 'the future'? What will happen if you put all the Palestinians in this built-up area? What will happen to them? Will these areas all become ghettos? This is a recipe for disaster.

UN responsibility

There was a clause in the UN agreement which said very clearly that the UN is responsible for seeing that the Palestinian state is established. They are obliged, and frankly we should bring this issue back to the UN. Not to Bush, not to Blair or Brown or Sarkozy; it has to go back to the UN because it is their responsibility. They should not leave it to us – Israelis and Palestinians – because there is an absence of symmetry. Israel is holding all the cards. Israel allows Abu Mazen (Mahmoud Abbas) to move from his house to his office, but he has to get permission. If he wants to go outside Ramallah, he has to get permission. If he wants to leave the country, he gets permission like anybody else. A head of state requiring permission! Imagine if Gordon Brown had to ask Bush for permission to leave his home.

I think there is only one way out. If you go back to justice for a moment, you can think of a solution. That

85

is where I think the Church should speak up. I started by saying that justice means being equal. Water – take all the water resources and divide them according to per capita. That is how you deal with it. Land – you do the same. But we accept the 22 per cent of Palestine – there should be resolution of the refugee problem according to Resolution 194 [the UN Resolution that spelt out the right of Palestinians to return].

So when Miss Livni (the Israeli Foreign Minister) goes to the United States and says we cannot allow one single refugee to come back to Israel because this would be a problem, our job is to tell her, 'Yes, Ma'am, but would Israel be willing to allow the refugees to take some part of the state of Israel, pre-1967, and add it to the Palestinian territory so it will not destroy Israel?' Let us exaggerate and say there would be a need for 1.5 million refugees. Divide them by seven (average family size), so you are talking about 200,000 households. Let us give each one one hectare. That is 2 million hectares – out of 27 million hectares. So it is about 8 per cent.

Eight per cent for the refugees

Eight per cent added to the Palestinian area and you solve the refugee problem, and you make Gaza and the West Bank contiguous because Gaza is so densely populated it needs fresh land. Give it part of the desert; with water it will become good. With the ten dunams (one hectare) of land, these people will start growing things to feed Israel. Only 2 per cent of Israelis in Israel contribute to the agricultural sector. Most of the workers in agriculture are not Jews. They are either Romanians, Filipinos, Thais or

Palestinians. Give us the land and the water, we will produce the best tomatoes that they want and sell to them. This will provide jobs. When people find jobs they will not become prey to Hamas. Instead of wasting our time in speeches we would be busy meeting the deadline for the next export. There would be progress. And yes, we are an agrarian society. With time, we will shift from agriculture to something else. But we need a quick way now to provide employment for a large number and the only sector that can accommodate us very quickly is agrarian.

So you get durable and sustainable peace. Why don't the churches say this is justice? If Jesus would rise today, he would say, 'This seems to me the only sustainable solution because it is justice.'

We are not the children of a lesser god

I want to see the wall fall. I want to be free to move. I want to see gardens rising, water in the taps. No checkpoints. That is what we need. The people who should raise this are the churches as they fight for justice. That is what they should be doing – asking for gardens, water, proper infrastructure and sewerage, proper humanity and dignity. This is God. These are the values of Christianity. It is not political. It is justice. I am asking for justice. We are *homo sapiens*. We need more than water and food. We are not the children of a lesser god.

So restore the ties between Jerusalem and Bethlehem. Stop the ethnic cleansing of Palestinian Christians. Let Bethlehem be open to the world. Let Santa Claus come without passing through Israeli checkpoints!

Witness 10: Mai Nassar
No light at the end of the tunnel

Mai Nasser is a lecturer in English at Bethlehem University.

Gilo settlement bombarded us with rockets

Many of my family have emigrated since 2000 – I am thinking about married cousins, nephews, immediate family.
Many have left because they cannot see any hope in the
future; many were affected by the wall and the second
intifada together because they lost their jobs, their cars
and their houses. I was one of them. We were attacked
from Gilo (a nearby Jewish settlement). I lived just opposite Gilo and they used to bombard us with rockets; the
first rocket was on my house, so we left the house we had
lived in for 23 years.

We lost property and my father's olive grove was
uprooted; 54 olive trees were uprooted. We used to sell
olives and oil, now we buy them. The trees were uprooted
for the sake of the wall; this happened three years ago.
So many people lost hope in the future; they lost their
income because they used to sell olives, for example my
elderly aunt.

We lost our freedom of movement

With the wall we lost freedom of movement. We cannot
go anywhere except in the Bethlehem region, and we can
drive round all the Bethlehem region in 15 minutes; I
cannot bear it. I am a mature person; I am not young any
more, I cannot imagine myself living somewhere else,
but there is no light at the end of the tunnel, whether
Christian or Muslim; so many have lost hope and left.

Don't let Bethlehem die

We are strangled between bars

Now culturally of course we have lost many things because of the wall. Imagine, my nieces and nephews do not know Jerusalem, and Jerusalem is a 10-minute drive. You get a permit for one day. You get humiliated at the checkpoint, you have to go through a body search, your handbag is searched, you go into rows and I always imagine myself in the rodeos in the United States – it is the same kind of place they put the bulls.

We are strangled between bars; it is very humiliating. It is torturing for children. After you go and see Jerusalem, Jerusalem is no longer the Jerusalem we knew, because it has lost many of its Palestinian inhabitants. So it is not the same Jerusalem that we had before the wall; even the spiritual part of it is lost in this process. So I am sorry that my nieces and nephews haven't had the experience of being a Christian Palestinian and going at Easter to pray in the Holy Sepulchre. We have lost all of this. It is part of our religion but also part of the culture. So we have lost this also.

The origin of our problem is the British

I see that the origin of our problems is the West; I am sorry to tell you it is the British. The British have affected the history of our region. They do not understand what is going on. Not that they are not smart enough, but now with globalization, Britain is one of the central powers, they are not helping us.

The public do not know much – they support whatever they find most visible. For instance, the Israelis have spread their cause and people are sympathizing with the Israelis more, and we are seen as the negative party in this conflict.

89

Part of the responsibility is on us, because we did not promote ourselves, we did not talk about our cause enough. The public do not know because they just see what is on TV. I have been to the West and I have visited America and Britain and there is not much on the news about our cause.

I went to the USA with Partners for Peace

I can tell you something from my observation, that the people in Europe are more aware of the conflict than the people in America. In America they do not know anything, they do not know where Palestine is; at least the British know that there is a conflict here. When I went to the USA, I went with Partners for Peace, which brings together people from the three religions with one vision. I was the Christian member in 2003, and we did about 65 events in 12 major cities in the USA. I am sorry to tell you that they did not know that there were Christians here; they did not know anything about Israel or anything about the Palestinians, they were so ignorant of everything. At least the British know that there is a conflict and I appreciate that.

I am a proud Christian Palestinian

To the churches I would say, 'Try to support us, and try to think of our cause', because in the coming decades all these churches here will be in ruins, and you will find maybe an old priest telling you that a Christian community lived here. I cannot visualize many Christians living here in the coming decades; I keep saying we are the last generation here.

I am a proud Christian Palestinian. I always say it. I always wear a cross. I am proud that I am Christian, I always tell my students I am respected here, I am not persecuted;

it is me who cannot tolerate it any more, it is not the people around me. That is what the West has to know, that we are not persecuted. Palestinians are Muslims and Christians, and we suffer together.

I do not have any hope

I do not have any hope. I stopped hoping a long time ago, because I kept being optimistic and what happened was the opposite. My grandfather died in 1955 and he was telling us that we had a piece of land at that time. He is dead now and we cannot reach that land. Now under the strict laws it will be confiscated, because no one from my family lives outside the wall, and my father had this dream of building on part of that land (my father died in 1998). I will die in the coming years, so there is no hope, I cannot see any hope. Things are getting worse every day.

For younger people I cannot give any advice. I will try to encourage them to stay, that is what I do with my nephews and my nieces, but I am not convinced of what I am doing! Because here there is no life; no life for any young person, virtually no life at all.

We cannot even dream now

My message to the Church would be, 'Help the Palestinians in general – and the Christians in particular', because the Christians need hope, need work. I am not begging for money, I am begging for them to create a dream, to create a future that any young person can live. There are certain things in life you cannot live without – we want security, we want safety, we want money, we want a future, and we want to dream like all other people in the world. We cannot even dream now. Even at night I have stopped dreaming. Believe me, I am telling the truth. This was not so ten years ago. Now I have stopped dreaming at night.

This last intifada and the wall have destroyed everything for us, the two things together. We stopped dreaming. And when you stop dreaming, this is so difficult. My message is: help us to have a future, to have a dream. Believe in our cause, try to influence your governments, try to influence the public so that they know we Palestinians are suffering. We are the victims. Stop victimizing the Israelis and crying when you see an explosion, because imagine someone who puts a belt around his waist and goes to explode himself – do you think that this idea was in his brain when he was born? It was not. I am not defending it, I am not supportive of these operations, but think of that person who goes and puts the belt on – he has no hope at all. If our young people had hope they would not do such acts. It is not that we like to kill people; it is being hopeless, and when you are hopeless you can do anything crazy.

Pray for the spirit of Christmas to return

I would tell the worldwide Church that there are still Christians. We are Palestinians. We are Christians. They do not know that Arabs can be Christians.

I am a Palestinian Christian. Amazing, isn't it, because you don't know that we exist; we have existed since Jesus was born here. We believe in Jesus, the same Jesus as you, but we do not have the spirit of Christmas because it was killed by the Israelis. We do not have people coming to Bethlehem on Christmas Eve. We do not celebrate Christmas because most of us do not have families to celebrate beside us as many Palestinians emigrated. Palestinians have not got the luxuries of Christmas. They cannot have a turkey or exchange jewellery, because this is beyond their budget. Please pray for the spirit of Christmas to return to Bethlehem because we do not have it any more. It will return with peace, by having security, by having a future, by having a dream of tomorrow. That is how it will come back.

If the British cared more, they would speak more...

I believe that Europeans are intellectual: they read a lot, they know a lot about our cause, they know who are the victims and who are the occupiers; but they do not care to say anything to anybody, they just know it. I believe that if the British cared more they would speak more and they would do more because they are smart people.

Witness 11: Salim Munayer
The uniqueness of Palestinian Christians

Salim is Director of Studies and a professor at Bethlehem Bible College and Director of Musalaha Ministry of Reconciliation. Salim is an Arab/Palestinian Israeli from Lydda, the city of St George. His family had been there for generations. They became refugees in their own home town in 1948; they are part of the few Christians (200) who found refuge in a church, and were able to stay. The rest from the same city were forced to move to Ramallah on the West Bank.

It is very discouraging

Looking around right now it is very discouraging. What we were hoping for a few years ago was a Palestinian state; this dream seems far away right now. The other aspect of discouragement is the direction in which both Israeli society and Palestinian society are moving. If you are a Palestinian Christian right now like myself with Israeli

93

citizenship and you were hoping that there would be a Palestinian state next to Israel, and that this would resolve some of the dilemmas, and if you were looking for equal rights in the state of Israel as Palestinian Arabs, it is all very discouraging.

The Christmas message of the vulnerable child

One message of Christmas is: do not be misled by people who have power right now; real power lies somewhere else. Who are the powerful? Who are the powerless? This vulnerable child who did not have a place to be born, he is the one who has more power than the most powerful ruler of that time. Augustus and Herod had power at that time; it seemed that they were in control of history, but in reality they were not. Are we able to look behind those things that are happening around us to see what God is doing here? Another message is that it is OK to flee. It is OK to be fearful. It is OK to find refuge. It is OK to ask for help. Mary and Joseph and baby Jesus, they found refuge in Egypt. Our human response to suffering, our human response to persecution, our human response to dealing with powerful rulers is that maybe sometimes we need to bend down, we need to move, but at the end of the day, they came back from Egypt!

Where is the western Church's theology of Palestinian Christianity?

I think there is a calling for the Church. The Church does not have a theology for Palestinian Christianity. That is my biggest problem. For instance, certain churches in Britain have a theology about Israel, whether you agree with it or not. They have a theology about Jewish people, whether you agree with it or not. But they do not as a church have a theology of Palestinian Christianity. We do not have a theology as to why Palestinian Christianity is important, why Christians need to be here, and how we can learn from their spiritual heritage of two thousand years of history. In essence, the reason the church outside needs to support, stand with, pray for and encourage the church here, is because God put this church here in history. So what is its role and responsibility and what can we learn about that? If we do not have a theology, we will not stand with the church.

There is something more than that even. It is Bethlehem. It is a place; it is history. Help Palestinian Christianity, help Christian Bethlehem, because of the biblical background, because it is history, because the existence of the church up to now from the early time to today has been on-going. Now this church is under threat of not being here any more. Bethlehem could be turned into a museum.

The uniqueness of Palestinian Christianity as a bridge between West and East

But there is something even more important; it is the uniqueness of Palestinian Christianity as a bridge between West and East, between Muslim, Jews and Christians. The uniqueness of the Palestinian church is that it can present to the Church a theological reflection concerning the land and theology. This is the reason why the Church of England needs to stand with the Palestinian church – for its uniqueness. For because even if you look at it from a theology of the land, the meek will inherit the earth. The land where Jesus was born, where Jesus taught, where Jesus did miracles, where he was crucified and rose again is important. The people who live in the land – their history – is important. But more than that, the questions that Palestinian Christianity is posing to the Muslims and the Jews as a minority among Muslims and Jews, are questions western Christians will not ask.

The most misunderstood Christian community

That is why it is important – we bring a dimension to what is happening here about peace and about justice. This is why Palestinian Christianity is important. It is challenging for Judaism, because for the first time in history since ancient times, Jews are sovereign in a land of a Christian minority. Before this Christians were dominant and Jews were a minority. How Muslims are treating Christians will reflect on relationships between Muslims and Christians in Europe and America. It is all connected.

The Palestinian Christian is the most misunderstood Christian community right now in the world. This community's only way to survive is the way of the cross because they do not have the sword. The way of the cross calls us to call people to reconcile to God and to each other. The cross calls us to be vulnerable and to empathize with the suffering of the people. At the same time, the cross calls us to forgive our enemies because if we do not forgive our enemies we turn out to be like them – this is our challenge here. If you do not let go of your grudges and forgive you become like the one you most dislike.

This is the liberating power of the cross. This is something unique that Palestinian Christians understand – the fullness of the cross – because they do not have power. So this community and its unique position in the place that God has put it in this time in history is very important for the Church worldwide.

Witness 12: Bishop Riah Abu El-Assal
Too many are leaving

Bishop Riah was the previous Anglican Bishop in Jerusalem. He is now retired and living in Nazareth, though constantly travelling to speak about the situation. I have talked with Bishop Riah regularly since first going to the Holy Land and I sat with him in his home in Nazareth, with his wife Suad and daughter Rania.

Many are leaving, especially from the Christian community. Already we have lost some 3,000 young people who emigrated to different parts of the world. Last October, different embassies issued 10,000 visas. If I were to examine the 10,000 I would find the majority are from the Christian community. Now there are reports of 50,000 new applications. Even my immediate family are talking about wanting to emigrate. I have lost the majority of my immediate family to the West. Who is left here? My children and myself. My children tell me, you brought us here because of two things, your commitment to the Church, to Christ certainly, and your commitment to the homeland. It seems we are going to be left with no homeland. So why stay? There is a feeling of hopelessness among the Christians. The number is dwindling and means have become very limited.

Our countrymen in Bethlehem are surrounded by a wall; I have to accept humiliation every time I cross out of Bethlehem in order to come back to Nazareth. It is painful. People may decide this is the end. We either pack and leave, or wait perhaps another hundred years until things work out for peace. Now this is not only true of the Christian community in Bethlehem, this is equally true of the well-off and educated of the Muslim community in Bethlehem. So this causes people to ask, what is the use of staying in Bethlehem when my children are already somewhere else in the world?

Do not stand far off watching

The wall is now almost complete. Look at Qalqilya. Qalqilya has two gates now; they can easily shut the first gate and then trap people between the two gates. In time of war they will lock the gates. Even in a time of quiet people cannot get to school. Every other week, they invade Nablus and kill two or three and take nineteen or twenty hostages. What is this? Where is the world? The world today is much like those who came from Galilee two thousand years ago, standing afar off at the crucifixion watching. Some of them may not be only watching, but counting how many times you have been whipped, counting the whips, but not feeling the pain. Standing afar off as our people in Bethlehem suffer. As our people in Gaza suffer.

My message for the churches at Christmas

My message for the churches at Christmas is, 'Stop mentioning the word Bethlehem unless you care about us.'

Stop singing 'Oh little town of Bethlehem' unless you come and visit its people, unless you do something about protecting the holiness of the place, and the Christian history of this wonderful place.

Why continue to sing for Bethlehem when Bethlehem is in prison? How can we sing joyfully when people are being killed, harassed and humiliated?

It is true that Jesus Christ did not find a place at the inn, but you are not told that he was humiliated, you are not told that he was stopped from entering Bethlehem.

I am sorry to say that the way the Church today relates to the Christian community in the land of the Holy One and to the people of Bethlehem, it causes me to wonder whether we are of the same family.

I ask the question, 'Are we really of the same family? What are you doing? Singing? Praying for peace?'

There is something wrong with us. Christians make up 2 billion people in the world, and we can't resolve the issue of Bethlehem.

Witness 13: Canon Naim Ateek
A Christmas message: 'Fear not!'

Naim is a liberation theologian, the founder and Director of the Sabeel ecumenical liberation theology group based in East Jerusalem. He is author of the book *Justice and Only Justice* (Orbis Books, 1989).

I think we need to challenge churches to be more courageous at Christmas; today more and more people have some knowledge about what is really going on in Bethlehem, yet fear makes people keep quiet.

I think the message of Christmas is 'Fear not!'

It is at the heart of the message of Christmas. What is holding people back is their fear. People are unwilling to take a stand and I think the message of the angels is still very pertinent.

We can tell our church members that as long as they are afraid they will succumb to the message of the oppressors. That is what the oppressors want them to do – to be silent, to be afraid; they try to intimidate them.

But the message of Christmas is 'Fear not'.

We have the good news, and the good news does not allow people to be encircled in a big prison. This is not good news. So it places greater responsibility on us to say, 'What is happening in Bethlehem today is bad news, not good news.'

One of the first sermons of Jesus was about release of the captives, and in Bethlehem today they are all in captivity – they are prisoners. If we do not speak up, who is going to speak?

How can we celebrate Christmas when people are in captivity – when Bethlehem is in prison?

And yet, in spite of all of this, I would stake my life and say my hope is in God. He is a God of hope. We are people of hope. Our hope helps us overcome our fear.

And we will continue to address these issues prophetically – as much as we can – until freedom comes.

Witness 14: Sawsan Shomali
Come back to your roots; be aware of your roots; have pilgrimages

Sawsan Shomali from Beit Sahour is a lecturer at Bethlehem University in modern American and British literature. She is also co-author of *Bethlehem 2000 – A Guide to Bethlehem and Its Surroundings* (Waldbroel, Flamm Druck, 1997).

The effect of the wall on education

The wall has affected our lives in all sorts of ways. As a teacher here I have to face this every day, especially in the morning when I give my 8 o'clock classes. Most of the students who come from Jerusalem arrive late because of the wall and the checkpoints. Buses are stopped, students have to step down, their identities are taken from them, they have to wait until they get their IDs back, and then the bus is allowed to move on. So the 8 o'clock classes never start on time because of the wall and the checkpoints.

Sometimes students cannot make it. For instance, the day before yesterday, the Israelis went into a village in the Bethlehem area and announced a curfew, and made some house arrests. Then the students were not able to leave and come to university on time.

Because of the wall, we are not having any enrolment from the north of Palestine; we have very few students that are from that area. There are more from Jerusalem, but most are from the Bethlehem area.

The wall cuts us off from Jerusalem, so we do not have many students from Jerusalem with is only ten kilometres away from Bethlehem, less than eight minutes' drive. Now it takes a student around an hour to arrive here, so some students are facing difficulties coming here every day; they prefer to go to other Palestinian universities in Jerusalem. The people from Ramallah or north of Palestine now prefer to go to Birzeit University, or one in Nablus or the Arab American University in Jenin. So the wall is affecting Bethlehem University and our enrolment.

If we end up having all our students from the Bethlehem area, then Bethlehem University will turn into a high school. The same students spend 13 years at school together, then they come to university and stay together. This is not the idea of a university. The students are not challenged by other people, nor by being exposed to other cultures, or other religions. So the idea of university will be missing because of this.

The effect of the wall socially

On the social level, I know that many young men and women were engaged to other Palestinians from Jerusalem and because of the wall, and because of the difficulty of obtaining Israeli ID or passports, they had to break up.

101

The other example would be the visiting of relatives. I have relatives in Jerusalem that I have not visited for the last 12 years, and I know many others are like me. I cannot get a permit to go into Jerusalem. Other people can get permits issued by different churches at Christmas and Easter for religious purposes. In my case I cannot get one. I am told that I am on the blacklist. For security reasons, I am not given a pass. So social gatherings, family gatherings, get-togethers are not possible with the wall between people who live here and in Jerusalem. Recently people were given permits to drive their cars across the checkpoints and go to the north of Palestine. It is possible, but it is not easy. Going to Jenin might be a three- to six-hour journey. Without the checkpoints and the wall, I would be there in a maximum of two hours. There are some cities that you still need a permit to get to, for example Nablus. If you do not have a permit, you cannot drive your car through the checkpoint there.

Worshippers around the world need to be aware of their roots in Bethlehem

There is a tendency now in Palestine of encouraging other Palestinians in the diaspora to come back to their roots. And the root of Christianity is Bethlehem. Christianity started here. So this is the message – to encourage worshippers around the world to be aware of their roots, either by informing them about the situation, or by encouraging them to have pilgrimages to Palestine, Bethlehem, Jerusalem and Nazareth.

They are running away from accepting human rights

I say, 'Knock down the wall. If the Israelis want their security, we also want our security. If they want to live in peace, we also would like to live in peace. Their excuse for building the wall is because of what they call 'terrorist attacks'. Fear is not legitimate because these attacks are a result of their pressure, their inability to understand the needs of the Palestinians and their rights. By building the wall they are running away from accepting human rights. So my message is, if they want to protect their people, we are people too. We are human beings too.

It is a wall of separation

By building a wall, they are saying there is no way for coexistence – it is a wall of separation. So if there is a wall, there is no way that these two people would live together. If they cannot live together, then there will be no peace. There will never be peace. I have relatives in Jaffa. I have relatives in Haifa. I have relatives in Nazareth; I cannot visit them, they cannot visit me. By building this wall, they are intensifying hatred; if there was no hatred, hatred has started to build up.

If they knock down the wall, that could be a very courageous step and maybe a sign of peace. This is the least they can do.

Witness 15: Hosam Naoum
The star keeps on leading us to Bethlehem

Hosam is a Canon of St George's Cathedral in Jerusalem and looks after the Palestinian congregation and their 9.30 Sunday service. He is also acting Dean of the cathedral. Up until recently he was also the vicar of the Anglican church in Nablus. He is an Israeli citizen from Galilee but his wife Rafa is from Nablus in the West Bank. Under Israeli law it is almost impossible for such a couple to live together unless they leave Israel, but then they will lose their Israeli citizenship.

Currently he has a permit for his wife Rafa to stay with him for one year, but this is an ongoing area of stress. (See my book, *Towards the Dawn* (SPCK, 2004), p. 109, Orna Kohn on family reunification.)

The future is dark

At the moment I think we live in a vacuum in the sense that it is a dead space where nothing is happening. The future is dark, and it seems that there is no hope. It seems that there is no vision for the future. On the Palestinian street the situation is not happy. What we see in the split between Fatah and Hamas is killing the last and only hope of the Palestinian people being together. We need one aim rather than an internal conflict – it is as if we now have two portions of the dream of Palestine. So it is all depressing and we cannot uproot Christians from this situation. It is not an easy life, and the challenges that face Christians here in this region are getting harder every day.

The wall of course is one of these challenges and it has really separated people from each other. People who live on one side of the green line are separated from those on the other side, and the people of Jerusalem are separated from the rest of the West Bank. I feel it now because I am the priest of this parish, the Church of St George's, and I see my own parish is struggling with this issue.

One-third of my parish live behind the wall

One-third of my parish live behind the wall. So this is one difficulty, one big challenge. Economically speaking, due to the political situation people are struggling to find security and to find a job. Because of the wall we have a new challenge – most of our parishioners are moving from around Jerusalem into Jerusalem itself, leaving their homes and apartments. They leave whatever they have and come and live in a room or two in Jerusalem in order to keep their residency, because otherwise the Israelis will take away their ID from them.

The hidden power in the equation

We have two kinds of pilgrims who come here. The first group see shrines and old holy places and they go back home; they will be encouraged for themselves in their own faith. The others will have the same experience as those pilgrims had but with one addition, that they have met 'the living stones'.

They meet their fellow Christians and their family members, and their lives are transformed into something deeper than just for their personal faith. They have experienced other people's lives, they have learned about others. They become committed to advocacy and they are people who are praying for us every day.

These pilgrims come here and their lives are touched by what they see. They go back home and they will always remember meeting Christians, Muslims and Jews. We all need prayers. But they remember this land and they pray for this land, and that is the hidden power in the equation. I do not expect them to change the whole world, but at the same time we feel that the more people come, the more we have links. I describe it as if every time a pilgrim comes a string is being connected between England and Jerusalem, between Washington and Jerusalem, between Auckland and Jerusalem, and one day these strings, these lines, will be so strong, maybe they can change something . . . maybe.

Christmas and Bethlehem –
the drama continues but the actors change

Christmas is a time to celebrate family life, to celebrate each other, to celebrate the reborn Christ in our midst.

I think we should always remember Bethlehem whenever we celebrate Christmas, especially at this time, because the story of the nativity is still alive in today's society and in Bethlehem. There are faults and fights in the story of the nativity, things darker than the image that we have with all the lights and all the candy. There is Herod and there are the children of Bethlehem – things that we should be worried about. Enjoy Christmas, but at the same time try very hard to make this enjoyment also touch other people's lives, especially those who live in Bethlehem, because over the years the drama continues but the actors change. I want the whole world to feel with the little town of Bethlehem. Our eyes will be focused on the manger. I think that we should go one step further and go beyond this wonderful atmosphere that we enjoy so much and go beyond our Sunday school theology.

The star keeps on leading us to Bethlehem and we need to follow the star. So how can we follow the star while we are in Britain or while we are in the United States? We could follow with our prayers. We could follow the star with our charity, with our advocacy. So how can we make this practice become real? Maybe by forming a link between a school in Britain and a school in Bethlehem, or a church here and one in Britain. Do something practical.

Witness 16: Bishara Awad
This is Bethlehem that received the Lord Jesus Christ

Bishara Awad is the President of Bethlehem Bible College. I have interviewed him for all of my books. The college is right by the separation wall inside Bethlehem.

The situation in Bethlehem is getting worse and worse by the day; many people of Bethlehem, because of the pressure, are just packing up and leaving the land altogether.

Bethlehem should be important to every Christian all over the world

For us as church leaders, this is very sad and very dangerous because what we are going to witness in the near future is Bethlehem where Jesus was born with no 'living stones' in it at all. This is why we have Bethlehem Bible College, but we would like to see the Church outside be more and more involved with Bethlehem. This is not my Bethlehem. This is Bethlehem that has received our Lord Jesus Christ. The Saviour of the world was born here in Bethlehem to save the whole world, so Bethlehem should be important to every Christian all over the world.

But I am very saddened to see that we here in Bethlehem feel that we are ignored; we are neglected by many of the people outside. Christmas comes and people outside sing these beautiful songs of Christmas – 'O Little Town of Bethlehem' and 'O Come Let Us Adore Him' – and yet the people of Bethlehem want to celebrate; they want to be happy, but the situation is preventing them.

So we want to see a change, and that change cannot only come from within. It has to come from outside. People are powerless. They can hardly do anything. We like to bring joy to the people. We like the people to celebrate. We like to bring gifts to the people of Bethlehem. There is so much the Church outside can do to bring life to what is left of the remnant of the people of Bethlehem.

Bethlehem Speaks

The world is losing its soul

We read the Bible every day and we pray together. We pray
for hope, we pray for peace. And we see what is happening in the whole world. It seems that the whole world is
slowly losing its soul and there is so much killing. There
is so much frustration and violence that is happening all
over the world. Where is the Christian message in all of
this? I think there is a moral responsibility, when people are
in need, when people are beaten up like the Palestinians.
We have completely lost everything. We have lost our freedom. We are like that man who was set upon by thieves
and left to die; we look to the West to be the Samaritans,
to come and help the remnant of the Christians here.

We would love to see the Church be more and more
involved; to save what is left of Christianity in Bethlehem,
in the West Bank, in Jerusalem, and in all of the territories.
We cannot let the Jewish state just dictate. They need to
hear an outside voice and maybe they will change some
of their tactics against the Palestinian community and
especially the Palestinian church.

The relationship between Christians and
Muslims is very good

I am proud to say that the relationship between Christians
and Muslims is very good. They are our neighbours and
they treat us well. We have now been here 28 years as
Bethlehem Bible College. We are in a very strategic area
in the centre of the town, in a place that is very busy. Across
the street from us is a refugee camp that has been here
since 1948. Behind us is another refugee camp. All of the
people in these refugee camps are Muslims and we have
never been harassed by the Muslim community at all. We
reach out to them. They are good neighbours to us and

108

we try also to be good neighbours to them. We want to be a light to them and to the rest of the community. Contrary to what we hear outside, we are not being harassed by the Muslims at all.

It is time that the conscience of leaders be awakened

I would really like to meet with political leaders whether in England or in America to tell them that the people who are living in Bethlehem and in the Palestinian territories have been badly treated for a number of years. We are losing numbers because of the ethnic cleansing that is going on. It is time that the conscience of these leaders be awakened somehow and a stop put to all the injustices.

We need to see leaders that are faithful to God and faithful to themselves, who really study the situation and understand both sides – Israeli and Palestinian – and see the injustices that have taken place against the Palestinians. There are Jews who see the injustices; what about our fellow Christians? They should also see these injustices. To the people of the United Kingdom and other countries and to the churches I say there are so many things that you can do for the people of Bethlehem.

I would be very happy to provide the churches with a list of church leaders and pastors so that maybe you could write a letter and encourage them. They need encouragement. Maybe you could send a small gift to their church members. Maybe you could have a sister-to-sister church relationship. This can be done. Come and encourage us as people of faith.

7

How do we respond?

Shine on (star of Bethlehem)
Shadow of death hides the light
As refugees seek safety tonight
And children who walk in the darkest of fear
Need a sign that hope is near
To bring light into the dark

Shine on, shine on star of Bethlehem
Shine as on that night
Shine on, shine on star of Bethlehem
Teach us to show your light

See that star shining bright
And pray that we may show the light
Of lives lived so conflicts cease
By learning to walk the way of peace
And bring light into the dark

Shine on, shine on star of Bethlehem
Teach us to show your light
Garth Hewitt

One of my concerns has been that as we sing about Bethlehem
each year we should say something about the community that
exists in Bethlehem, because the very theology of the incarna-
tion means that this is where God reached down to humanity

in a special way, in humility, and lived in a context where God affirms the value of every human being. Consequently, I wanted to make sure that there was always material for people to use in their churches that could bring this incredible message of God's valuing of human beings into the context of Bethlehem today. God chose to become human into a context of poverty and occupation. There is an extraordinary relevance to how the body of Christ, namely the Church, should be responding to the Bethlehem community both in our services and in our action.

In the light of the story of our witnesses, how should we respond to what is going on in Bethlehem and other areas of the West Bank and Gaza? As several people have stressed, the most valuable thing is to go and visit. At Amos Trust, we take a pilgrimage every year, and we can recommend others who make sure that visiting the 'living stones' is a key part of pilgrimage. Going behind the wall and seeing first-hand is (a) a tremendous moment of awareness-raising, and (b) gives real encouragement to the Palestinian community.

Second, we can then tell the stories ourselves and make others aware of what we have seen or what we know. Writing letters and campaigning are very important, both in terms of informing our members of Parliament and also our church leaders.

Third, there may be ways we can support, not only in giving to projects which is very important to keep the different institutions and organizations going, but also by buying olive-wood goods and olive oil that comes from Palestine, and other goods that help to support the economy of Palestine.

Furthermore, it is important in our services, in our prayers and meditations, to show our commitment to the Palestinian church and the Palestinian community and also our commitment to peacemaking and peace and security for both Palestinians and Israelis. For several years now at Christmas Amos Trust has put out a 'Bethlehem Pack' in conjunction with the Interfaith Group for Morally Responsible Investment (IMRI). This is a group of Christians, Muslims and Jews who work together on certain specific campaigns to raise awareness of issues of disinvestment and investment. The Bethlehem Pack contains prayers for Advent, voices from Bethlehem, song lyrics, alternative carols and meditations. I will include resources from our Bethlehem Packs at the end of the book so there is practical material that can be used particularly in the Advent/Christmas season to help people focus on the Bethlehem area. Also use some of the words of our witnesses about Christmas. I have included some extra comments from them in the Bethlehem resource material.

At the end of the day, our witnesses have reminded us, 'Don't forget us. Come and visit us. Tell our story.' They stress that now is not the time to keep silent. It is the time to speak up, or it will be too late for them and the community of Bethlehem. It is time for us to speak with courage, as Archbishop Trevor Huddleston did over South Africa as he called the Church and the world to wake up to what was happening in apartheid South Africa in the 1950s. His clarion call was the book *Naught for Your Comfort* (Collins, 1956). The title was taken from G. K. Chesterton's 'Ballad of the White Horse':

> I tell you naught for your comfort,
> Yea, naught for your desire,
> Save that the sky grows darker yet
> And the sea rises higher.

Trevor Huddleston said:

What I shall try to avoid is that most common and persistent error in all such assessments – the attempt to be impartial. By this I mean that I shall write this book as a partisan, for I believe that Christians are committed in the field of human relationships to a partisan approach. I believe that, because God became man, therefore human nature in itself has a dignity and value which is infinite ... Any doctrine based on racial or colour prejudice and enforced by the state is therefore an affront to human dignity and *ipso facto* an insult to God himself.

Towards the end of his book he says:

The immediate future must be dark: darker, I believe, than it is at this moment of writing. There is no sign whatever that there is a weakening in the application of the apartheid policy: just the reverse. There is a kind of buoyant confidence ... that, in spite of world opinion, in spite of 'liberalists', clerics, communists and agitators, the African people are accepting and will continue to accept the medicine handed out to them in larger and larger and more frequent doses. . . . Opposition . . . is presently at a low ebb, the lowest that ever I remember. 'The seduction of power' is having its effect. But that this effect is temporary, I am absolutely convinced.

He ends his book by saying:

It is for the church to proclaim fearlessly, in season and out of season, the truth of the gospel: and to recognise that that truth is revolutionary ... The way of apartheid is a denial of the very foundation of the gospel itself. It is a return to the question, 'Am I my brother's keeper'; a forsaking of the question, 'And who is my neighbour?' It is a denial of charity, and therefore a denial of God himself. Nothing will persuade me otherwise ... and I KNOW the solution ... It lies in the simple recognition that ALL men . . . are made in 'the image and likeness of God': that in consequence each PERSON is of infinite and eternal value. . . . Only we who, in our ordinary daily life, accept and at least try to act upon these truths, know how easy is the answer. 'If thou hadst known, even thou at least in this thy day the things which belong unto thy peace. But now they are hid from thine eyes.'

This was the prayer Jesus said as he wept over Jerusalem. Our prayer must be that these things will be hidden from view no longer, so that the truth of what is going on is revealed, that Bethlehem is not hidden nor the rest of the West Bank or East Jerusalem or Gaza. Let us believe that 'a further shore is reachable from here' and let us pray and work for 'the longed for tidal wave of justice [to] rise up', to use the words from Seamus Heaney's poem with which I began.

John O'Donohue died as I was writing this book, a wonderful storyteller and poet, and I would like to end with a prayer of his taken from his most recent book, *Benedictus: A Book of Blessings*.

A Prayer for Peace

As the fever of day calms towards twilight,
May all that is strained in us come to ease.

We pray for all who suffer violence today,
May an unexpected serenity surprise them.

For those who risk their lives each day for peace,
May their hearts glimpse providence at the heart of history.

That those who make riches from violence and war
Might hear in their dreams the cries of the lost,
That we might see through our fear of each other
A new vision to heal our fatal attraction to aggression

How do we respond?

That those who enjoy the privilege of peace
Might not forget their tormented brothers and sisters.
That the wolf might lie down with the lamb,
That our swords be beaten into ploughshares

And no hurt or harm be done
Anywhere along the holy mountain.

8

Bethlehem resource material

Introduction

This material has been produced by the Amos Trust as a resource to assist with the planning of services and carol concerts for Advent and Christmas, in the hope that these events will reflect the reality of life in present-day Bethlehem.

The material includes:

- Advent prayers to go with the lighting of candles.
- Prayers – some specifically on Bethlehem, as well as general prayers for justice, peace, and even hope in a situation that is looking hopeless.
- Poems and meditations.
- Christmas song lyrics (how to obtain the music/recordings).
- Alternative Christmas carol lyrics – for use in more informal carol events.
- Suggestions for practical action.

There are also a range of recent photos of Bethlehem and the surrounding wall, which can be provided as jpegs for use in services (contact <info@amostrust.org>).

In some services maybe just one prayer will be suitable, in others a campaigning action might be appropriate. Whatever you do, keep Bethlehem on the agenda at Christmas – not in a romantic way, but by raising awareness of the reality of the suffering in a land once known as holy. Some of the song lyrics are included earlier in the book, in which case the page number is given. There are also further comments about Christmas contained in the body of Chapters 4 and 6 on pp. 38, 87, 92, 94, 98, 99, 105 and 107. My thanks to Chris Rose, Wendy Ross-Barker, Stephen Leah, Ramani Leathard and Deborah Maccoby for their contributions to the alternative carols and prayers.

Advent prayers

Prayers and thoughts for the Sundays of Advent about the land of the Holy One and the struggling 'little town' of Bethlehem (suitable for the time of candle-lighting).

First Sunday of Advent

A prayer for Bethlehem

In this time of Advent may we remember the people of Bethlehem, especially our Christian sisters and brothers.

> From this little town the Prince of Peace came,
> but today they know no peace.
>
> Imprisoned by a wall, with land taken,
> being economically strangled, many have fled.
>
> Yet the church longs to continue its witness here as it
> has done through the centuries.
>
> As we light our Advent candle today and we start
> preparing for our journey towards Christmas
>
> May we not forget Bethlehem – and also continue to
> pray for all the suffering communities of the Holy
> Land.

Garth Hewitt

Second Sunday of Advent

A prayer for justice and peace in the land of the Holy One

> Living Lord, ignite in us a passion for justice
> And a yearning to right all wrong.
> Strengthen us to work for peace
> In the land we call Holy:

for peace among Jew, Christian and Muslim
for reconciliation between communities
for harmony between faiths.

Inspire us to act with the urgency of your quickening
    fire,
for blessed are the peacemakers
they shall be called the children of God.
    Ramani Leathard (Christian Aid and Amos trustee)

Third Sunday of Advent

*A prayer about the wall of separation in a land
once called holy*

Living God, in Jesus you broke down the wall of
    division.
We see other walls that divide in our world
Like the separation wall that cuts into the heart of
    Palestine
Imprisoning a whole community –
Cutting them off from one another, from their work,
    from hospitals
From education and from places of worship.

God of liberation, strengthen them in their struggle
May hope be born again from the Prince of Peace's
    birthplace in Bethlehem
And throughout this land once called holy.

May Palestinians find justice at last
So Palestine and Israel can both live in peace –
Both live securely – both live in freedom
Without walls, without checkpoints, closures and
    curfews.
May we realize the great message of hope that all are
    chosen or none

We're all in this together –
One God, one community, one hope, one future.
Garth Hewitt (from Making Holy Dreams
Come True, *SPCK, 2006)*

Fourth Sunday of Advent

A thought from a Bethlehem Christian for hope and light in the Holy Land

Despite the difficulties in our lives, we will rejoice at the birth of Christ at Christmas. Taking our inspiration from the story in the Bible of Herod's massacre and the flight to Egypt of the holy family.

The inspiration comes from knowing that despite being born into those dark days, amid the harsh Roman occupation, and despite the fear that must have gone with the family as they escaped to another country, Jesus did return and was able to spread his ministry of peace and love.

We are living in a similar situation over two thousand years later, behind the apartheid wall and under the harsh occupation by the Israelis, and many Palestinians are escaping to other countries. But we are persevering and will celebrate Christmas with the message of hope and deliverance that Christ has planted in our hearts.

We pray that through the miraculous birth of Christ we will see the wall go and change into a bridge of understanding between the two peoples living here.

Our prayer is that through mutuality, inclusivity and reciprocity, the road to reconciliation will conquer all kinds of fears, paranoia and injustices, and the Holy Land will once again be the source of hope and light.

Zoughbi Zoughbi (Director of Wi'am Conflict Resolution Centre, Bethlehem)

Bethlehem today

Behind the wall: Christian voices speak

These words are from Christians living in Bethlehem today or elsewhere in the Holy Land. One could be used in place of a reading in a carol service or read in a sermon slot.

The Christmas story in Bethlehem, Palestine

It is sad that the Christmas story has become a moral-less tale of three huts and three camels and three magi, and so it is very romanticized. It is about Santa and it is about the tree and it is about this and about that. While nothing of this is actually mentioned in the Christmas story. So all of this was made up, basically.

The Christmas story is a story about a very concrete town with very concrete people with very concrete issues and problems and the Christmas story is about a child who is a refugee.

He is a refugee in Bethlehem; he is a refugee in Egypt.

The Christmas story is about Herod who is killing children, fearing that children are challenging his empire.

The Christmas story is about good tidings brought to shepherds who are outcasts.

So in that sense I think that Christmas nowadays is everything else but about Christmas.

It is more about business and marketing than really about the real issue.

Dr Mitri Raheb (Pastor of Lutheran Christmas Church, Bethlehem)

Bethlehem is going down

Bethlehem is going down, so we need compassionate listening because in hearing there is healing.

We need prayers and exchange visits as the Palestinians are being collectively punished for their democratic choice. Our hope is in you – we see God in your faces, in your prayers, in your words. I shiver with hope when you come.

In Bethlehem, we are hostages to fear and paranoia. Less than 0.05 per cent get permits for travel; consequently there is no freedom of movement and therefore no freedom of religion.

Displacement of anger is increasing domestic violence and 90 per cent of children are showing signs of trauma. There are many psychological problems and not enough psychiatrists.

Over five hundred families have left Bethlehem in the last five years (i.e. three thousand people) and Israeli fundamentalists are creating more and more settlements. We live in a pressure cooker, which is a recipe to make you leave if you can. In the long run the Israelis want the land without the people.

Rachel's Tomb has been surrounded. There were over eighty shops nearby, most of which have now closed. The wall is squeezing everywhere and land is being taken.

We do not get post in Bethlehem, or if we do it is severely interfered with. For instance, we had some Disney videos sent from the United States for the children. They did not arrive for months; when they did arrive, only the boxes came and the videos were taken out. When we asked the reason, they said it was 'for security'.

Israel worships the new Golden Calf of security; meanwhile the ethnic cleansing of a people is going on, and so in Bethlehem we will end up a museum.

We call for the world, especially the Christian world, to recognize its collective responsibility for Bethlehem and what is happening to the West Bank and Gaza.

We want you to help us maximize our prophetic voice and we call for positive investment in Palestine – invest in relationships and faith.

We are passing through the Via Dolorosa. I believe in resurrection and hope; my family have lived here for over four hundred years, so I hope my kids will be able to live peacefully and enjoy their lives and have a safe haven they can call home.

I hope the wall will collapse and there will be no more judgement on the basis of colour, gender or race.

We live in a demoralized society . . . how can we transform the garbage of anger into the flower of compassion?

Zoughbi Zoughbi (Director of Wi'am Conflict Resolution Centre, Bethlehem)

Where to find the baby Jesus today

People in every generation have to decide which side to take.

At the first Christmas, there were the Herods and there were the people who were waiting for the coming of the Lord, the righteous people, the humble people.

Today Christians need to come to Bethlehem and they need to decide whether to be on the side of the new Herods, the new Pilates, the new Pharaohs, or whether they are going to be on the side of Christ.

To be on the side of Christ is to be on the side of the oppressed in Bethlehem.

Today, the best place to see the baby Jesus is to go to a refugee camp rather than the Nativity Church.

That is where you see the reality of what is happening on the ground; you see real life, and not just tourist attractions.

So I would say, look at things in a Christ-like perspect-ive to see the reality of Bethlehem and stand with the child of Bethlehem and do not stand with Herod.

By our silence, we are accepting the status quo which is devastating to the people of Bethlehem, devastating to the chance of peace between Israelis and Palestinians.

What is happening in Palestine has its ripples all over the world.

So if we want peace in the world, which is the Christ-mas message, then we need to stand in solidarity with those who are suffering in Bethlehem.

Alex Awad (Dean of Students at
Bethlehem Bible College)

The calling of Christmas

Christmas is the business of God becoming flesh – God becoming real – touchable – visible to people.

For God's sake, make your Christian calling become flesh, touchable, felt, in terms of your relationship with your brothers and sisters in this part of the world.

For me that is Christmas.

Christmas is allowing your words and your Christian call and your Christian stand, your Christian prophetic voice to become real.

So take your place, and see your role, in all of this and support the Church in this part of the world.

It may be far away from you physically but you cannot ignore your role spiritually, because if we believe in the one body of Christ, it is your responsibility as much as it is my responsibility.

If Christmas is not this commitment then I think we are fooling ourselves, making it a nice little play on a stage for kids and that is it. It stops there. It has no ongoing relevance.

So make your Christian calling become flesh.

Fuad Dagher (Vicar of St Paul's, Shefa'Amr, Galilee)

I wish you would remember us

At Christmas I would like to convey hope to the churches and to wish them a very Merry Christmas and a Happy New Year.

I want you to sing these beautiful carols and to lift yourselves and your souls up to the Lord, but at the same time I wish that you would remember us, the 'living stones' who are here.

We are in Bethlehem, and we are your brothers and sisters.

We would love to celebrate together this coming Christmas, and to know that you really care about us, and that you care about the Church here in this land;

And that you care enough to see that the Church will continue to exist in the land where it all started.

Bishara Awad (President of Bethlehem Bible College)

Prayers

Prayer for peace in the wounded places

Vulnerable and wounded God –
We pray for peace in the wounded places of our world.
Some have problems so great that we are tempted to
  despair
And feel they can never be solved.

But may we never lose hope.
We are the community of resurrection
So lift our spirits – renew our vision
And particularly give us strength
To support the peacemakers in those places
That are suffering.

May we be those who refuse to walk by on the other
  side –
And be those who build links of love and support.

Vulnerable and wounded God
We pray for peace in the wounded places of our world.

> *Garth Hewitt (from* Making Holy Dreams
> Come True, *SPCK, 2006)*

Making holy dreams come true (A Christmas prayer for Bethlehem)

What have they done to the 'Little Town'?
Imprisoned it in a concrete wall
Bethlehem – once a holy city
Trapped inside a ghetto wall.
Here where angels sang of peace
Where love and hope were born anew
Once surrounded by a heavenly host
Now surrounded by a concrete view.

Yet people crushed and hidden away
Still celebrate on Christmas Eve
Lighting candles for the child –
They still remember – still believe.
So light a candle this Holy Night
For Bethlehem and Beit Sahour
And for all the people caught inside
That cold and grey prison wall.

Longing for a world of peace
Where all are treated equally
Where all can recognize their worth
Where all can live with dignity –
Where all can join hands with neighbours
Whether Muslim, Christian, Jew
And find a way to live together
Making holy dreams come true.

> *Garth Hewitt (from* Making Holy
> Dreams Come True, *SPCK, 2006)*

Light in darkness

Light of Christ, enter into the darkness of oppression
   and humiliation
With your warming glow . . .
Fragile and vulnerable, as when you came new-born in
   a manger.

Light of Christ, enter into the darkness of indifference
   and ignorance
With your startling brilliance . . .
Bold and challenging, as when you confront injustice
With the powerful weakness of self-giving love.

> *Wendy Ross-Barker (Advent 2002)*

Prayer for Christmas Eve

O God – Christmas Eve is such a wonderful time
Lights and laughter
Excitement and expectation
Candles and carols
Family and friends
Food and fun
And we try to stop to pray –
Or read a Christmas poem of John Betjeman
And I'm always moved as we come to those words
'And is it true? And is it true . . .
The maker of the stars and sea
Become a child on earth for me?'
As he asserts that if this is so 'nothing can compare
    with this truth'
And I find it hard to carry on because there is nothing
    more to say
Because it reveals that you are the God
With such a precious love for humanity –
So we must cherish human rights
You are the God of humility – made visible in the
    ordinary person
In the everyday ordinariness of life
You are the God of the forgotten and insignificant –
    and therefore there is hope for all
And we too are shown how to live

And you are the God of Bethlehem today –
You would choose it again precisely because the world
    thinks it is
Insignificant and its people are of no value
So the angels would sing again to say 'here God is at
    home'

And the wise would be surprised again saying – 'here
   God is at home'
And shepherds, and carpenters making olive-wood gifts
And tour guides with no work, and drivers of coaches
   for pilgrims
And innkeepers and all the community – women,
   children and men –
Crushed, humiliated, invaded and imprisoned
Can stand up tall with confidence and proclaim 'here
   God is at home'
Because you have shown your character in
   Bethlehem –
You affirmed humanity in Bethlehem . . . and still do
   today
And that is the message of Christmas Eve.

> *Garth Hewitt (from* Making Holy Dreams
> Come True, *SPCK, 2006)*

More holy dreams

God our friend and companion –
Each faith has a longing to follow you – to find the
   holy.
Each faith has some words close to the golden rule
That Jesus gave us –
'Do unto others as you would have them do to you'.
Each faith tries to deal with ego
So we learn to walk the humble road
And become better neighbours.
We have a dream – rooted in the scriptures
That mountains will be brought low and valleys lifted
   up –
That mountains of injustice, human rights abuse and
   oppression

Will be brought low so that a society of justice,
   humanity and caring
Will become a reality.
That instead of increasing the divisions and bitterness
We will see walls come down and neighbourliness
   increase
That hope will rise and peace will come
So arms sales fall and resources are shared
So all will see every human as equal
And treasure each one as made in the image of God
Then holy dreams will become true
And hope become a reality.

Garth Hewitt (from Making Holy Dreams
Come True, *SPCK, 2006)*

Meditations and poems

Not so, this Christmas

Did shepherds once guard sheep
On hills near Bethlehem,
Fearing only wild animals?

Not so this Christmas –
When the danger that lurks in the hills is a
    camouflaged tank.

And were those shepherds made fearful
By bright lights which turned out to be angels
And a loud noise which became
A heavenly song to the glory of God?

Not so this Christmas –
When the sound of the sky is the roar of helicopter
    gunships,
The light, the bursting rocket.

Did shepherds once walk freely
From those hills down to the town
Where folk slept soundly – apart from that group in the
    stable?

Not so this Christmas –
When the route is blocked by checkpoints
And a towering concrete wall,
And citizens, walled in, fear for themselves and for their
    children.

Is that family still there – poor, vulnerable?
Mother, father and the child
Who will know the suffering and sorrow and death,
Yet through it all, bring hope.

Bethlehem Speaks

People of God, go afresh to Bethlehem
In the light of reality.
Occupied then – occupied now
Innocents slaughtered then – and now.

Go and see the child who will grow
To be the man who cries for justice,
Who dies to bring new life.

He invites us to follow him.

© Wendy Ross-Barker (November 2003)

Children of God

Child of God, you came to Bethlehem,
Born into poverty and vulnerable
In a city under occupation . . .
You came –
And innocent children were slaughtered
At the command of a king
Who saw you as a threat to his security.

Children of God, living in Bethlehem,
Forced into poverty and vulnerable
In a city under occupation . . .
He comes –
Where innocents are slaughtered
In the interest of security . . .
Sharing the pain.

© Wendy Ross-Barker (Advent 2002)

The following poem takes Psalm 23 as its inspiration, and was written as a celebration of the work of the International Solidarity Movement, Christian Peacemaker Teams and other Peace Observers who accompany and protect Palestinians in their homeland from illegal settlers and foreign soldiers.

Palestinian Psalm 23

The Lord is our Peace Observer,
We shall be protected.

He comes with us as we harvest in our fields.
He stays with us to report any violence against us
His presence guarantees our safety.

He escorts our children to and from school
For they are the future, our treasure.

Even though we walk in the shadow
Of the illegal Apartheid Wall
We will fear no violence, for you are with us.

Your pen and your email, they defend us
You report the truth to the world.
You give us hope, despite the presence of the occupiers.
You show that our lives are important, that people do
care.

I pray that freedom and peace may soon be ours,
All the days of our lives
And we shall dwell in the Holy Land forever.

Stephen Leah (2007)

Where is that light that shines in the darkness?

Is it hidden behind a 25ft-high separation wall?
Is it trapped without a travel permit?
Is it labelled a fundamentalist, a terrorist?
Or is it weeping over Abraham's children?

Where is that light that shines in the darkness?

Is it hidden behind a wall of indifference?
Is it trapped behind self-interest and greed?

Is it labelled a victim, of famine, natural disasters and
    war?

Or is it crying out for justice, truth and compassion?

Where is that light that shines in the darkness?

Is it hidden by a mother's arms?
Is it trapped – a refugee, a displaced person?
Is it labelled as the illegitimate child of a teenage
    mother?
Or does it come creeping into our midst?

Where is that light that shines in the darkness?

Is it hidden by the lens I see through?
Is it trapped by my self-image?
Is it labelled by my prejudice and mistrust?
Or is it slowly coming into view?

Chris Rose (Amos Trust)

Did Rachel laugh?

(Written on the annexation of Rachel's Tomb.)

Did Rachel giggle as Jacob, a stranger, rolled the stone away
from the mouth of the well for her? Did she laugh at her
sister's substitution on her wedding day, or did she, as I
suspect, find that distinctly unfunny?

Did she laugh behind Jacob's back when God renamed
him Israel, or was she too bitter about her infertile state,
or too resigned to his 'struggles with God' to care? Were
there tears of joy at the birth of Joseph and did the proud
parents laugh together at his first attempts to walk?

And what of Israel's tears at Rachel's death, as he gave
thanks for another new son yet lost the woman he had
loved? Did his tears water the ground as he buried Rachel
outside Bethlehem on the Pilgrims' road, a covenant

reminder of the journey between the Patriarchs' graves and Jerusalem, the future City of God?

Yet in death Rachel weeps and refuses comfort, weeping for the innocent slaughtered in Bethlehem.

Rachel, do you still weep and find no comfort? Do you still weep for the end of innocence? Do you weep for Bethlehem's children whose future is denied them? Do you weep as their childhood is eroded – as they witness their land being confiscated, their livelihoods uprooted and their families dispersed? Do you weep for Bethlehem's Palestinian children?

But why should you cry for them? It was Esau, Jacob's brother, who married Ishmael's daughter. Jacob chose you to be the mother of the children of Israel. Your grave is Judaism's third most holy site. It is a shrine for a million visitors a year and a place where infertile Jewish women come and weep, beseeching you to intervene with God.

Has there been so much pain that you cannot find it in your heart to care for the Palestinians? Have the centuries of anti-Semitism and persecution been too much to bear? Have you become as hard and cold as the concrete separation wall that cuts you off from Bethlehem's residents?

Rachel, 'the ewe', do you rest more easily now that you can no longer see the shepherds' fields where angels pronounced 'Peace and goodwill to all people'? Do you, like some English village, delight in the new bypass road that ensures that your visitors are only Israel's descendants, those who come to honour you?

Or do you miss the travellers on the pilgrims' road, those who journey from Hebron to Jerusalem? Do you miss familiar Arab faces passing by your tomb on the way up to Jerusalem as they have each year since the first Pentecost? Do you miss the Palestinian graves and homes, which have been your companions for centuries? Do you recognize that their DNA profile is closer to yours than many scattered through the Diaspora?

But if you cannot cry for the Palestinians then weep for Israel's children. As peace slips from them, beneath the clatter of armoured vehicles and helicopters' blades, and the explosions of homemade rockets.

Weep, that the dream of the return has been marred by fear and distrust. Weep, that power has once again overtaken compassion. That vengeance has triumphed over humanity. Weep as their leaders follow their name-sake and grasp more and more of God's blessing – the gift of the land.

Weep because the wall that surrounds you will not bring peace, weep for the future generations who will have to act as wardens, jealously guarding God's blessing. And weep with those women who come to you begging for God's blessing in them. Begging to feel new life, yet fear that their blessing may all too soon be tragically taken away, in an endless cycle of violence.

Rachel, weep! Until all recognize that you have cried enough.

Chris Rose (Amos Trust)

Songs

Here are some songs to use as meditations:

- They've cancelled Christmas (The wall must fall) (see p. 20)
- Hidden from view (see p. 11)

(An album of songs by Garth Hewitt about Bethlehem is being released to coincide with the publication of this book. It is called *Hidden from View*. Details of availability will be on the Amos Trust website <www.amostrust.org/resources> (and then click on 'music'). A recording of at least one of the songs will be available on the website and on YouTube.)

The songs that follow use traditional hymn tunes.

Advent and Christmas

O sad and troubled Bethlehem,
We hear your longing cry
For peace and justice to be born
And cruel oppression die.
How deep your need for that great gift
Of love in human form.
Let Christ in you be seen again
And hearts by hope made warm.

While morning stars and evening stars
Shine out in your dark sky,
Despair now stalks your troubled streets
Where innocents still die.
And Jesus, child of Mary,
Whose love will never cease,
Feels even now your pain and fear,
Longs with you for your peace.

137

[Handwritten marginal notes:]

We give thanks for the opportunity to-day to hear directly from our Christian friends from Bethlehem, the work of the B. Star Charitable Society. Through the work of the society may Christ to day be seen again and hearts by hope be made warm.

Bethlehem Speaks

Amazingly and lovingly
Jesus, the child, has come
And, brought to birth through human pain,
Makes broken hearts his home.
He comes to comfort all who weep,
To challenge every wrong
And, living with the weak and poor,
Becomes their hope, their song.

© Wendy Ross-Barker (2001) Tune: Forest Green

Christian people, raise your voices

Christian people, raise your voices,
Tell of Bethlehem today,
Suffering while the church rejoices,
Fearful, where the peace-child lay.

When you share the Christmas story
Let the truth of it be heard.
Look beyond the tinsel glory;
Listen for the Living Word.

Hear him in his people's weeping
Feel their longing and despair.
Threat of harm disturbs their sleeping,
Wake, God's people, be aware!

© Wendy Ross-Barker (2004) Tune: Stuttgart

Alternative Christmas carols

The following 'alternative' carols have been created to reflect the current situation in Bethlehem, the impact of the wall and the isolation of the people.

O come all ye faithful

O come all ye faithful
Those who care for justice,
O Look ye, O look ye at Bethlehem.

Come and behold it,
Under occupation.
O come let's not ignore it,
O come let's not ignore it,
O come let's not ignore it –
Tell the world.

Sing all ye people,
Sing in indignation,
Be with the citizens of Bethlehem.

Sing out for justice,
Freedom from oppression.
O come let's not ignore it,
O come let's not ignore it,
O come let's not ignore it –
Tell the world.

O come all ye faithful
Those who care for justice,
O Look ye, O look ye at Bethlehem.

Deborah Maccoby (Just Peace UK, 2002)

Bethlehem Speaks

O little town of Bethlehem

O little town of Bethlehem
Imprisoned you now lie.
Above thy deep and silent grief,
Surveillance drones now fly.
And through thy old streets standeth,
A huge illegal Wall.
The hopes and dreams that peace will come
Are dashed in this year's fall.

O morning stars together,
Look down upon this crime.
The people sing to God the King
But justice, who can find?
Yes, Christ was born of Mary,
God's love remains supreme.
But mortals sleep as children weep,
Their pain is never seen.

How silently, how silently,
The world and Church protests.
As checkpoints grow and towns confined,
As settlers steal and rest.
No ear may hear the outcry,
As Israel's Wall is built.
While meek souls muse, Apartheid rules –
We speak or share in guilt.

O Holy Child of Bethlehem,
Give strength to us, we pray.
Cast out our fears and open eyes.
O give us voice today!
We stand against injustice,
The Occupation must end.

May justice rule our Lord's birthplace,
May now Christ's peace descend.

Stephen Leah (2007)

The following is a version of 'In the bleak mid-winter', reflecting on the practice of the occupation of holding expectant mothers at checkpoints on their way to hospital.

At the army checkpoint

At the army checkpoint,
Queues had stood for hours.
Cars stood still in gridlock
Alongside watchtowers.
Guards barked out their orders
Under hot sunshine.
At the army checkpoint
In Palestine.

Amongst all the traffic,
On a car's backseat,
A woman lay in labour,
Midwives she must meet.
At the army checkpoint
A layby place sufficed;
A precious little baby;
A mother's special child.

Businessmen and tradesmen,
May have gathered there.
Dust and noise and car fumes
Filled the noonday air.
But in this mother's anguish
Doctors were denied;
Soldiers stopped their travel
And the precious boy; he died.

Bethlehem Speaks

What should my response be
Weak though I am?
If I were a statesman
I would bring a plan
If I were more famous
I'd do all I dare.
Yet what I can I'll promise,
I'll show that I care.

Stephen Leah (2007)

Taking action

Here are some practical ways that churches and individuals can get involved in supporting people in Palestine.

Supporting Wi'am's Christmas campaign

For many families in Bethlehem Christmas is no longer a time of celebration, but one of despair.

At this time it is hard too for families to celebrate when parents see little hope for the future, when there is no money for presents and when the New Year brings school bills that they will not be able to pay.

Amos supports our partner Wi'am's annual Christmas appeal. They will be holding a community Christmas celebration, with theatre, music, games, during which they hope to give up to 1,500 children a gift towards their education. They will also be supporting the elderly.

Selling olive-wood carvings

Owing to a decrease in tourism and the wall, craftsmen in Bethlehem are no longer able to make a living from their work carving olive wood.

Please contact the Amos Trust for information on running an olive wood stall in your church or community, supporting the people of Bethlehem directly by selling this beautiful hand-carved olive wood. Contact <info@amostrust.org> for more information.

Selling Zaytoun olive oil

Zaytoun works to find a marketplace for Palestinian produce in the UK, supporting farmers. More information about becoming a Zaytoun representative, selling olive oil and soaps, can be found at <www.zaytoun.org>.

Disinvestment

By encouraging those who have their money invested in companies that are benefiting from the occupation and the wall, such as Caterpillar, to withdraw their funding. At present the Church of England still has shares in Caterpillar. Please contact the Inter Faith Group for Morally Responsible Investment (IMRI) if you would like further details on disinvestment: IMRI, All Hallows on the Wall, 83 London Wall, London EC2M 5ND.

Pilgrimage

Most important of all, come and visit the 'living stones'. Amos has an annual pilgrimage each June. For further information, contact: Amos Trust, All Hallows on the Wall, 83 London Wall, London EC2M 5ND. Tel. 020 7588 2638. Email: <info@amostrust.org>. Website: <www.amostrust.org>. Charity no: 29259.

To keep up to date with news from Israel/Palestine, visit the International Middle East Media Center (IMEMC) website <www.imemc.org> for daily updates, and the websites of two human rights organizations – one Israeli and one Palestinian – for statistics: B'Tselem at <www.btselem.org/English> and Palestinian Centre for Human Rights (PCHR) at <www.pchrgaza.org>.

Wall xiii nearly nine metres high
This to allow our faiths to be seen as great again p7
Cited rocket attacks on Bethlehem 88
Prayer for spirit of Christmas + Bethlehem 93